W9-BZA-821

"Schultze's highly recommended book offers a practical road map for becoming a 'servant speaker' who serves the audience as a 'neighbor.' By reclaiming Augustine's vision, *An Essential Guide to Public Speaking* provides an important antidote to today's self-serving rhetoric in public speeches and the media."

Linda S. Welker, communication consultant;
professor, Northern Kentucky University

"Today's emphasis on skill over virtue is ruining public discourse. Schultze has come to our aid, succinctly combining the richness of rhetorical theory with a Christian perspective on stewardly discourse, making the classical ideals of wisdom and eloquence accessible to adults of all ages."

Nneka Ofulue, professor of communication studies, Eastern University

"Quentin Schultze has done it again! This special book, written by one of the most original and profound authors I know, takes a fresh look at public speaking as 'servant speaking.' My students love his call for communication that builds meaningful relationships rather than just performances or arguments. His retelling of Augustine's own transformation into a servant speaker is beautifully told and highly relevant for today. A must-read for everyone who wants to use speech to serve rather than to manipulate audiences."

Kathleen O. Sindorf, professor of communication and media studies,
Cornerstone University

"For a long time I have been looking for a short, inspiring book that not only talks about the skills of effective speaking but also revives the art of public speaking as a virtuous practice. *An Essential Guide to Public Speaking* does just that. It calls us to reclaim Augustine's vision of ethical, effective speechmaking and shows us how to do this in today's diverse world."

Mary Albert Darling, professor of communication, Spring Arbor University

AN ESSENTIAL
Guide to
PUBLIC
SPEAKING

SERVING YOUR AUDIENCE
WITH FAITH, SKILL, AND VIRTUE

QUENTIN
SCHULTZE

Baker Academic

Grand Rapids, Michigan

© 2006 by Quentin Schultze

Published by Baker Academic
a division of Baker Publishing Group
P.O. Box 6287, Grand Rapids, MI 49516-6287
www.bakeracademic.com

Second printing, March 2009

Printed in the United States of America

Library of Congress Cataloging-in-Publication Data
Schultze, Quentin J. (Quentin James), 1952–
    An essential guide to public speaking : serving your audience with faith, skill, and virtue / Quentin Schultze.
        p.   cm.
    Includes bibliographical references and index.
    ISBN 10: 0-8010-3151-6 (pbk.)
    ISBN 978-0-8010-3151-9 (pbk.)
    1. Rhetoric—Religious aspects—Christianity. 2. Public speaking—Religious aspects—Christianity. I. Title.
BR115.R55S38 2006
808.5′1—dc22   2005037933

Thanks to Linda Welker, Randall Bytwerk, Judi DeJager, Susan Pearson, Dave Buehrle, James Zwier, Brian Fuller, Helen Sterk, Nate Baxter, Chris Smit, Ruth Remtema, and the summer 2005 Workshop in Communication participants for their helpful comments and suggestions. Special thanks as well to the many persons who have invested in the Arthur H. DeKruyter Chair for Faith and Communication at Calvin College. Finally, thanks to God for the gift of Dr. DeKruyter, a gifted and faithful public speaker who by grace learned how to serve his audiences near and far, young and old, within and beyond the walls of the church. I am honored to dedicate this book to him, with additional recognition of Gladys's faith and love, which have nurtured him to success beyond human measure.

Contents

Introduction   9

1. Speaking in the World   11
2. Naming Responsibly   21
3. Addressing Challenges   33
4. Listening Well   45
5. Crafting Artfully   57
6. Speaking Truthfully   73
7. Being Virtuous   85

Appendix A: Checklist for Preparing a Speech   97
Appendix B: Checklist for Topic Research   99
Appendix C: Checklist for Audience Research   101
Appendix D: Using Slideware Wisely   103
Appendix E: Form for Evaluating Speeches   105
Appendix F: Sample Speech Outline Elements   107

Notes   108

INTRODUCTION

During the last thirty years, I have spoken regularly at businesses, professional conferences, schools, churches, conventions, and civic meetings. I have also appeared on many broadcast programs as a news source, commentator, and media critic.

Yet I was a shy child who suffered from social phobias. Speaking publicly was the last thing I imagined doing later in life. When I became a college teacher, I felt inadequate, like Moses: "Lord, send Aaron."

Public speaking is inevitable. We may need to give eulogies, lead group discussions, pray publicly, present awards, participate in civic meetings, and much more.

Unfortunately, the materials available for learning how to speak publicly have become excessively technical, focusing on skills without paying adequate attention to purpose and ethics. The biblical context—speech as a gift and a responsibility for the service of our neighbors—has nearly vanished.

This bias is unfortunate, because Christians historically contributed some of the most important insights on public speaking. Early Christians discerningly adapted speech practices from the ancient Greeks, who founded rhetoric (the art of persuasion).

By the time of Augustine in the fourth century, however, the art of rhetoric had become largely self-serving. Augustine, trained as a rhetorician before his conversion, eventually concluded that Christians needed to save rhetoric from insincere practitioners who (1) taught and practiced deception, (2) equated good rhetoric (eloquence) solely with audience impact, and (3) believed that the real, inner character of a speaker was largely irrelevant in contrast to how an audience perceived that speaker.

For the sake of church and society, we should reclaim Augustine's vision of rhetoric, which is fitting for servants of God in a needy world. Many governments, businesses, and other organizations need leaders who speak with honesty, integrity, and civility. Professions ought to nurture responsible as well as effective speech. So should schools, churches, and families.

This book reclaims public speaking as a noble practice for Christians. I encourage readers to become servant speakers who (1) faithfully serve audiences as neighbors, in the biblical sense, (2) are virtuous speakers, and (3) skillfully use verbal and nonverbal methods. Faith, virtue, and skill are the keys to servant speaking.

None of us knows when we will be called on to speak. Once my wife and I attended a wedding where we barely knew the groom and had never met the bride. We were invited because the groom happened to meet the bride when he was in our neighborhood to advise us about interior decorating. During the reception, the groom asked me to speak about our role in getting them together. How could I refuse such a gracious invitation?

So there I was, with minutes to plan an impromptu speech. What should I say? How should I say it? Then it dawned on me that I was just a messenger. God was the one who had really brought the bride and groom together. So I warmly offered a few thoughts about God's grace.

I feel the same way about this book. I never set out to write about public speaking. The more I spoke over the years, however, the more I felt called to encourage and teach others this important art. As stewards of God's gift of speech, we are all called to be servant speakers, skillfully offering our verbal and nonverbal messages as living sacrifices in the service of our neighbors and to the glory of the Lord.

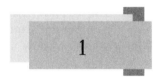

SPEAKING IN THE WORLD

During his Harvard commencement address in 1978, acclaimed novelist and former Soviet dissident Aleksandr Solzhenitsyn said that the Western world is losing its civic courage. He warned that "from ancient times the decline in courage has been considered the first symptom of the end" of civilizations. Solzhenitsyn suggested that the root problem might be the West's growing love of personal pleasure at the expense of public responsibility.[1]

Since we Christians are called to reach out to our neighbors in love (Lev. 19:18; Matt. 22:39), we should be courageously involved in God's world. We are created to serve others with all our God-given gifts. Therefore, we are called to be responsible, courageous speakers who use the gift of speech to serve God and neighbor—to be servant speakers.

As Augustine (354–430) pointed out, however, Christians' social involvement invariably creates tensions between what he called the city of God and the city of man.[2] We are members of both the eternal body of Christ and temporal social institutions such as businesses, schools, and governments. We are responsible for serving not only our churches but also our families, neighborhoods, cities, workplaces, and nations.

The biblical way of addressing this tension is to live *in* the world without being *of* the world. Christians are called to transform their minds so that they can discern the difference (Rom. 12:2). Accordingly, servant speakers are called to speak the truth in love without conforming mindlessly to the ways that the wider society communicates. Paul even says that we should learn to become all things to all people (1 Cor. 9:22). Our public speaking, for instance, must be sensitive to the rights and perspectives of those with whom we disagree while remaining true to our values and beliefs. What we say and how we say it are part of our witness to the world.

Democratic Discourse

Democratic societies, in particular, offer servant speakers the freedom to identify with the city of God while speaking responsibly within the city of man. As British statesman Winston Churchill told the House of Commons in 1947, "Democracy is the worst form of government except for all the others that have been tried from time to time."[3] Democracy gives human beings the freedom to shape their own futures by collaborating with other citizens.

The gift of speech equips citizens to live responsibly in communities of their own making. We can listen and learn together, conduct trade, worship, debate the issues of the day, and participate in many other communication practices that are vital to the functioning of society. Open public discourse enables us to identify our differences of opinion and to strive together to resolve conflicts in the name of the common good. It also enables us to enjoy relating to one another. Speeches have always been among the most influential, educational, and enjoyable forms of public communication.

Therefore, we should use the gift of communication wisely to form public associations such as neighborhood groups, city commissions, and nonprofit clubs. We should attend meetings, discuss and debate policies, choose leaders, and serve one another. Such voluntary associations have long been a part of the moral and political fabric of healthy societies.

This is why democratic discourse is so critically important in a free society. For self-determination to work, citizens must enter all social institutions as responsible communicators who listen carefully and speak well. The overall health of a republic depends on citizens responsibly participating in neighborhoods, service organizations, and the like. The freedom of speech is a gift to be used responsibly, not just a right to be protected legally. After all, free societies are the exceptions rather than the rule in history. They must be nurtured.

Speaking *in* Society

We as Christian citizens take up our public responsibilities partly through the gift of communication. The word *communication* derives from the same Latin root for *community* and *common*. Language, in particular, enables us to *commune* with one another for the sake of defining and addressing our shared interests as citizens.

The risk of speaking as a Christian in a pluralistic society is nothing new. Early Christians had no voice in public life and were routinely silenced and sometimes killed. When Christianity became the official Roman religion three centuries after Christ, believers faced a remarkably complicated situation: how to communicate publicly with unbelievers who disrespected the church and sometimes even despised Christ followers.

The biblical answer is one of the great themes of Scripture: merciful, loving justice. The prophet Micah said, "And what does the LORD require of you? To act justly and to love mercy and to walk humbly with your God?" (6:8). Imagine this command applied to speech. The Lord requires us to speak justly and to love merciful speech and to speak humbly with our God.

As most Christians now understand, the right of one group to express itself publicly must be matched by the freedom of others to do likewise. Communicative justice—giving all citizens a voice in public life—becomes meaningless if citizens do not value responsible listening and speaking.

Therefore, public discourse has to be open to citizens of all faiths and no faith. Christians, too, have to learn how to make

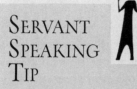

Servant Speaking Tip

Learn how to dialogue responsibly with people from other faiths as well as agnostics and atheists.

their cases as persuasively as possible, even sometimes to defend their faith.

For example, Solzhenitsyn's commencement address, covered by major media around the globe, implicitly expressed a Christian perspective. After reviewing evidence of the Western world's moral poverty, he concluded the speech by saying, "No one on earth has any other way left but—upward."[4] Although Solzhenitsyn remained true to his convictions about the moral ravages of radical individualism and excessive materialism, he sought to communicate a faith perspective while respecting cultural and religious pluralism. Solzhenitsyn appropriately used the freedom of speech to advocate for universal moral standards in modern societies. He sought what all servant speakers seek

> The humanistic way of thinking, which had proclaimed itself our guide, did not admit the existence of intrinsic evil in man, nor did it see any task higher than the attainment of happiness on earth. It started modern Western civilization on the dangerous trend of worshiping man and his material needs.
>
> Aleksandr Solzhenitsyn, *A World Split Apart*
> (New York: Harper & Row, 1978), 49

when they enter public life: an honest hearing from a charitable audience. Not intending to dismiss or offend those who disagreed with him, Solzhenitsyn was true to democratic discourse as well as his faith.

Philosopher Richard Rorty says that citizens should never use religious language in public life. He calls such language a "conversation stopper" that leaves no rhetorical room for political negotiation. If a believer says that all abortion is murder, for instance, he or she eliminates space for discussing other points of view.[5]

Rorty is partly correct. Even within churches, religious rhetoric can stop dialogue cold. Nevertheless, singling out religion is unfair, since *any* deeply held conviction, religious or otherwise, can stifle public discourse. A secularist can be just as dogmatic as someone who believes in God. In fact, totalitarian leaders generally eliminate freedom of speech so they can squelch dissident voices. Moreover, a religious or nonreligious speaker still has to make a credible, convincing case in order to persuade others to agree.

The dogmatic nature of some secular as well as religious public discourse is becoming increasingly obvious to many social critics. Playwright Václav Havel, who was jailed for years under the post–World War II communists before becoming president of the liberated Czech Republic, says that the Western world is going through "a great departure from God which has no parallel in history." He warns that we are "living in the middle of the first atheistic civilization" and must rediscover a responsibility "higher" than human beings.[6]

Communicating responsibly in society as servant speakers requires us to avoid overly moralistic or dogmatic language. In the church, we should openly share our deepest beliefs founded in Scripture. But in society, from civic debates to business presentations, we need to learn how to listen well and to speak convincingly with those who hold opposing as well as similar convictions. Then we can better adapt our verbal and nonverbal communication skills to a wide range of nonchurch settings in order to serve the broader society well.

Speaking Up for Others

Sometimes we have to speak up because others are being treated unjustly by people or institutions—including churches. Christians have inherited a long history of biblical truth tellers, from Moses to Dietrich Bonhoeffer. We know that God has given us the gift of speech primarily to serve others rather than to advance our own selfish agendas.

When to Speak Up in Society

- to defend the essentials of the faith (apologetics)
- to empower the voiceless excluded from public discourse (communicative justice)
- to expose wrongdoing when direct confrontation with offenders will not work (whistle-blowing)
- to repair others' wrongly damaged reputations (ethos restoration)

Two biblical examples are especially remarkable. Moses protested God's apparent injustice. He stood before God at Mount Sinai and advocated for the emerging Jewish nation, even though it had failed to live up to its covenant obligations (Exod. 32). He appealed publicly to God to forgive the people. Similarly, while on the cross, Jesus asked the Father to forgive his foolish murderers (Luke 23:34).

Much of the church remained sympathetically silent if not apathetic during Hitler's reign in Germany. Bonhoeffer instead spoke compassionately against the racial and political idolatry of that era, criticizing "silent witnesses of evil deeds" and faulting the church for fighting "only for its self preservation."[7] He was arrested, imprisoned, and executed toward the end of the war.

A Christian friend speaks up for persons who probably have been wrongly imprisoned because of witnesses' perjury. After thoroughly reviewing the evidence with wise attorneys, he speaks on behalf of these victims to the courts and media. He also addresses church and community groups to gain their financial and prayer support. Clearly, he is a servant speaker.

The ancient Hebrews recognized God's calling to speak up for others. Leviticus warned that people would be held responsible for failing to testify publicly about something they knew (5:1). Sometimes silence is a sin.

Martin Luther King Jr. and many other preacher-activists spoke courageously about the rights denied African Americans during the 1960s and 1970s. Among them were faithful black women who joined the public cries for racial justice. One of them, Septima Poinsette Clark, recalls that "the civil rights movement would never have taken off if some women hadn't started to speak up."[8]

Knowing when and how to speak up is not always clear-cut. We should avoid sticking our noses too earnestly into others' business. In addition, servant speakers will face overlapping as well as conflicting obligations to church, employer, God, friends,

> If we do not raise our voices against war, against hate, against indifference—who will? We speak with the authority of men and women who have seen war; we know what it is. We've seen the burnt villages, and devastated cities, the deserted homes, we still see the demented mothers whose children are being massacred before their eyes, we still follow the endless nocturnal processions to the flames rising up to the seventh heaven—if not higher.
>
> a speech delivered in 1981 to soldiers who liberated the Nazi concentration camps during World War II; Elie Wiesel, *From the Kingdom of Memory: Reminiscences* (New York: Schocken, 1990), 162

government, and many more groups. Paul tells the Romans to respect and obey governmental authorities (Rom. 13), but there are times when we are called to speak out against those who abuse their power and authority, whether in church, work, or government.

Speaking in Multicultural Communities

Few of us live in close-knit communities or economically independent nation-states. Transportation and communication technologies bring us into contact with people from other religions and cultures. Schools, cities, professional associations, and churches often face incredible linguistic and cultural challenges.

How can we work, dwell, and learn with those who are not like us? How can we appreciate the benefits of diversity without giving up our own beliefs and faith practices, such as mealtime prayer, weekly worship, Sabbath observance, and witnessing to our faith? How might we translate our faith into community service, business savvy, and political action without coming across to others as deceptively evangelistic or self-righteously close minded?

We can tackle these kinds of issues by learning how to communicate as servants of a God who has created all persons in his image and likeness. When we listen to and speak with others, we dialogue with persons who have just as much intrinsic value as we do, no matter how deeply we disagree with them or how much we misunderstand one another. From a biblical perspective, our oneness as human beings trumps our cultural and racial differences.

Moreover, cultural differences often are opportunities for mutual learning and serving. Churches historically borrowed cultural practices from outside the congregations. There are no culturally exclusive congregations in North America; every church owes much to previous Christian groups, to the saints of old and today who worked out their faith amid their own multicultural challenges and opportunities. They had to learn how to speak faithfully so they could simultaneously be holy (set apart) and socially engaged communities. Today's struggles over appropriate worship styles and fitting political activism are age-old issues that every generation of believers has to address.

The gift of speech equips us to participate faithfully in different cultures and subcultures. We can interact with neighbors, form community service organizations, and contribute to the vitality of public and private schools. Sometimes we will make major mistakes, such as apartheid in South Africa and congregational segregation in the United States, but we cannot live faithfully without listening and learning outside as well as inside the church. God's Word calls us beyond our comfort zones into all the world (Mark 16:15), where we learn by listening and influence by speaking.

This kind of open, discerning communication is at the heart of public speaking for Christians. The metaphor of the lone street preacher, ranting and raving at all presumably sinful persons who walk by, is hardly the place for us to begin as faithful public speakers. Some of these preachers probably are called to shout the gospel anonymously from busy street corners or college walkways. For most of us, however, a better metaphor is the servant speaker who listens not just to God but also to audiences. We are called to be slow to speak and quick to listen (James 1:19). In other words, we need to know what we are talking about and to whom we are speaking in this multicultural world.

Conclusion

Solzhenitsyn was probably correct: Modern democracies do need to look "upward" for truth and civic courage. Moral chaos easily slips into selfishness, whereas responsibility can blossom into service. Surely we Christians have learned from other cultures and inherited from Scripture an understanding of freedom that is eminently compatible with our faith as we seek to serve others in multicultural democracies. Some of the highest democratic principles—such as liberty, justice, and truth—can be good for the flourishing of all human beings.

The ancient Greeks and Romans gave the Western world an important rhetorical legacy by focusing on the use of speech to pursue the common good. Democracy today depends on citizens, including Christian citizens, who are committed to this noble endeavor of serving one another freely with the gift of speech.

Augustine inherited this rhetorical tradition even as he reformulated it imperfectly for the church in his era. As the next chapter suggests, he is probably Christians' best link between the ancient rhetorical tradition and modern democracy. Although he initially rejected the art of persuasion as evil, the Spirit did not let him off the hook so easily. A native North African serving in the Roman church, Augustine adapted ancient Greek and Roman rhetorical practices to the needs of multicultural congregations in a pluralistic society. Along the way, he realized that God was calling him to courageously anchor his oral communication skills in faith and virtue so that future generations could learn from his life story.

Naming Responsibly

When Augustine became a Christian in 386, he faced a dilemma: what to do with his previous training as a secular rhetorician. Augustine already was an accomplished speaker and a well-known teacher of rhetoric (the art of persuasion). But as a new Christian, he doubted that he could continue to practice a profession dominated by self-seeking deceivers who loved flattery and sold their rhetorical skills to nearly any buyer.

For a while, Augustine gave up teaching and practicing the craft. But as he grew in wisdom, eventually becoming a priest and then a bishop, he concluded that Christians are called to serve others by responsibly using the gift of speech.

The Gift of Language

Every human being inherits a remarkable linguistic capacity. Contrasted with animal signaling, human speech is incredibly complex. We do not merely speak; we encourage, ridicule, promise, pray, deceive, and so much more.

We can even speak without saying anything. Medieval monks, who lived by vows of silence, developed elaborate sign languages

SERVANT
SPEAKING
TIP

Learn to listen and speak well so you can communicate better in other media as well.

to communicate inaudibly. Signing is just as powerfully nuanced as verbal language.[1]

Whatever form it takes, language is our primary mode of communication. Writing and other means of human interaction depend on the backdrop of words, which people begin using before they can read and write.

Prior to Jesus Christ's birth, the ancient Greeks and Romans developed elaborate rhetorical theories and practices. Public speaking thrived in courtrooms, assemblies, theaters, and civic celebrations. Rhetorical trainees learned by repeating what instructors taught and then by debating others. Aristotle (384–322 BC), Cicero (106–43 BC), and others transformed rhetoric into an important academic subject and a professional practice that are still being studied, appreciated, and developed.

For the next two millennia, the theory and practice of rhetoric shaped many professions, including drama, teaching, politics, law, and preaching. Early rhetoricians distinguished a few essential purposes for rhetoric related to the legal, political, and ceremonial needs of the day—the most common venues for public speech. But it was Cicero who summarized three purposes (or goals) for public speaking that Augustine later adopted as well: to teach, to delight, and to move.[2] Adapting those three for today, we could say that three important purposes of rhetoric are: (1) to *inform* an audience about a topic, issue, or skill, (2) to *please* (or delight) an audience, and (3) to *persuade* an audience to adopt particular beliefs or to take specific actions.

These three basic purposes can be combined in various situations to serve an audience. For instance, a good college lecture might inform, persuade, and please students at the same time, even though the fundamental purpose of the lecture is to teach. Similarly, a fitting eulogy might inform attendees about the deceased person's life, persuade the attendees that the deceased was a good person, and delight the attendees with a few stories about the deceased person's humorous adventures in life. In fact, to some extent all speeches should inform, please, and persuade audiences. Therefore, the real differences have to do with matters of degree and focus. Every speech needs to have a primary purpose among the three, both to help the speaker prepare the speech and to help the audience understand how to respond.

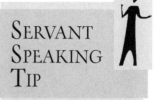

SERVANT SPEAKING TIP

Use terms such as *rhetoric* and *oral rhetoric* to refer to the art of skillful public speaking.

There have always been many ways of accomplishing these purposes for particular audiences. For instance, Jesus entered a society in which itinerant orators traveled by sea and road, speaking to audiences representing various social classes, religions, and cultures. Knowing his audiences perfectly, Jesus skillfully used verbal and nonverbal messages, such as writing sinners' initials in the sand (John 8:6). His rhetorical techniques included sayings, parables, and questions: "Who do you say I am?" he asked Peter (Luke 9:20).

A few decades later, the apostle Paul began his missionary excursions in the Roman Empire. Living out his conviction to "become all things to all people," Paul adapted the gospel to many audiences (1 Cor. 9:22 NRSV). In Athens, he persuaded like a philosopher. In Antioch, he taught as a fellow Jew. He wrote to various churches audience-focused letters (epistles) that were presented orally, similar to the way Scripture is read during worship nowadays.[3] Eventually, those letters became part of the Bible and are used by preachers today to instruct, persuade, and even please or delight congregations.

Many of the great theologians and leaders in the history of the church also served as public speakers who wrote about rhetoric. In addition to Augustine, they include Tertullian, John Wesley, Martin Luther, and John Calvin. We can still learn from their fine examples of preaching and teaching.

The archbishop of Constantinople, John Chrysostom (347?–405), who began his rhetorical education at the age of twelve, believed that an educated Christian should know how to speak well. Otherwise, a Christian's acquired wisdom could be miscommunicated, resulting in spiritual misdirection, errant Christian practice, and false or ineffective witness. Chrysostom realized that even a believer who knows God's Word must be able to express such insights clearly and persuasively for the church to benefit.[4]

PAUL ADDRESSES A GREEK AUDIENCE IN ATHENS

While Paul was waiting for them in Athens, he was greatly distressed to see that the city was full of idols. So he reasoned in the synagogue with the Jews and the God-fearing Greeks, as well as in the marketplace day by day with those who happened to be there. A group of Epicurean and Stoic philosophers began to dispute with him. Some of them asked, "What is this babbler trying to say?" Others remarked, "He seems to be advocating foreign gods." They said this because Paul was preaching the good news about Jesus and the resurrection. Then they took him and brought him to a meeting of the Areopagus, where they said to him, "May we know what this new teaching is that you are presenting? You are bringing some strange ideas to our ears, and we want to know what they mean." (All the Athenians and the foreigners who lived there spent their time doing nothing but talking about and listening to the latest ideas.)

Paul then stood up in the meeting of the Areopagus and said: "Men of Athens! I see that in every way you are very religious. For as I walked around and looked carefully at your objects of worship, I even found an altar with this inscription: TO AN UNKNOWN GOD. Now what you worship as something unknown I am going to proclaim to you."

Acts 17:16–23

He practiced what he preached, earning the name Chrysostom, which means "golden mouth."

Like all Christians from the time of Christ to the present, we have to rediscover the legacy of good, audience-serving speaking.

COMMON SPEECH SITUATIONS

- presenting to coworkers
- praying during worship
- leading a tour
- coaching a team
- testifying in court
- giving a eulogy
- teaching a class
- introducing a speaker
- celebrating an event

Each of us is born into a world in which contradictory words and meanings compete for our attention. We hear conversations at the dinner table, on the playground, via television and other media, at church, and in classrooms. We grow up realizing that the world is composed not merely of physical objects but also of questions and answers, invitations and promises, criticisms and praises. All of this can be incredibly confusing. Yet we are called to serve faithfully in this world of mixed messages.

When we attend a lecture, for instance, we should be able to use our own values, beliefs, and knowledge, including our knowledge of rhetoric, to judge *what* is being said. We also should be able to understand *how* it is being said and the *ways* it is affecting us and others. Then we need to be able to explain our thoughts to others so we can discuss and evaluate our conclusions.

An accomplished Christian philosopher learned during childhood to analyze "speeches" at home on Sunday afternoons. After church, his extended family would gather for dinner and discuss the morning's sermon. Invariably, this conversation led to biblical and theological discourse. Those experiences convinced him that words, ideas, and expressions have consequences. So he eventually became a philosopher.

As Augustine studied Scripture and reflected on his own rhetorical training, he concluded that Christians should "exercise and habit a most skillful use of words and an abundance of verbal devices."[5] He encouraged believers to imitate the eloquence of King David and Paul. Largely as a result of Augustine's persua-

Paul Addresses Jews in Antioch

Standing up, Paul motioned with his hand and said: "Men of Israel and you Gentiles who worship God, listen to me! The God of the people of Israel chose our fathers; he made the people prosper during their stay in Egypt, with mighty power he led them out of that country, he endured their conduct for about forty years in the desert, he overthrew seven nations in Canaan and gave their land to his people as their inheritance. All this took about 450 years.

"After this, God gave them judges until the time of Samuel the prophet. Then the people asked for a king, and he gave them Saul son of Kish, of the tribe of Benjamin, who ruled forty years. After removing Saul, he made David their king. He testified concerning him: 'I have found David son of Jesse a man after my own heart; he will do everything I want him to do.'

"From this man's descendants God has brought to Israel the Savior Jesus, as he promised. Before the coming of Jesus, John preached repentance and baptism to all the people of Israel."

Acts 13:16–24

sive arguments, the fifth-century church began adapting ancient rhetoric to its own good purposes rather than rejecting it outright. Augustine's book *On Christian Doctrine* (or *On Christian Teaching*) still encourages Christian pastors and teachers to speak wisely and well. It is one of the most widely read books ever written about how a Christian teacher should interpret Scripture and speak about it responsibly.[6]

"Response-able" Speech

The ancient Hebrews recalled how the Creator God first commanded Adam to name the animals. This kind of dialogue—God speaks and people obediently reply—became the biblical model for faithful speech.

Human communication was meant to be based on humans' "response-ability" to God's commands. In fact, the Hebrew word for "listen" derives from "obedience." Good speakers must first be obedient listeners so they know what they are talking about.

Adam's naming had at least two aspects: (1) defining reality in tune with God's Word and (2) being accountable to God as well as to others. Both are important for us today.[7]

Defining Reality

Adam gave the animals names to signify their distinctiveness. Each species deserved its own defining label in tune with God's ordered creation. A "horse" is not a "cow." A "human" is not a "horse."

Words can be much more than labels for things. Linguistic naming makes all kinds of additional distinctions. Some words express ideas: "Truth" is not "falsity." Others are verbs: "Promising" is different from "blaming."

When we use language, we often express various views of reality. For example, we define who God is and what he is like. If we are obedient, we define God's name above all others regardless of what people otherwise claim (Phil. 2:9).

Like Adam, we are called to define reality in tune with God's Word, not according to our own whims or interests. We define God as God, animals as animals, sin as sin, and so on. We have the freedom to define truth as falsity or to make a promise we do not intend to keep, but these are examples of irresponsible naming. When we deliver a speech to an audience, we define reality *for* them. This might be why teachers, in particular, are held to such a high degree of accountability in Scripture (James 3:1–2). According to their authority, they define reality for students (2 Cor. 11:4).

Perhaps most amazing of all, God uses the languages we create to communicate with us. We, in turn, use the same languages to communicate with God as well as with one another.

Being Accountable

Moreover, Adam was accountable to God, not merely to himself. He defined reality under God's authority, not his own (Gen. 2:19). Although he could name the animals freely, Adam recognized that he was created to be a God-accountable namer.

Actor Sydney Poitier recalled that, although his father was one of the poorest men in his Caribbean village, the elder Poitier had earned a good name among his neighbors. Consequently, the young actor sought to uphold his father's name. "Every time I took a part," said the actor, "I always said to myself, this must reflect well on his name."[8] Poitier wanted his public career to reflect positively on his father.

We human beings are like actors in God's story. Our principal role is to follow our playwright's lead. After all, the setting and the script are *his* gifts for *our* good. But the playwright has given us the freedom to improvise from his script, the Bible. As we study Scripture's "story" with other faithful speakers, we learn together how to be accountable to the playwright.

Without the script, we tend to speak irresponsibly. We wrongly aim to make a name for ourselves in tune with our own self-serving view of reality. With God's Word, we know we are called to be servant speakers who use the gift of speech to love God and our audience-neighbors as ourselves. A linguistic neighbor

"Christian" Speech

- defines reality in tune with the Word of God (John 7:18; 1 Pet. 4:11)

- demonstrates accountability to neighbor, self, and ultimately God (Eph. 4:25; 1 Pet. 4:11)

- imitates Jesus and his godly followers (1 Cor. 11:1)

is not just someone who lives nearby but anyone we can serve by using our language skills.

The calling to be servant speakers includes far more than spreading the gospel. All our verbal and nonverbal naming should serve God and neighbor. In fact, language enables us to tune into others' needs and to learn how to meet those needs. Such needs may be as common as entertainment, as indispensable as encouragement, or as complex as education.

All verbal and nonverbal language equips us to work together responsibly as servants in God's world. As Paul puts

SERVANT SPEAKING TIP

Speak responsibly, knowing that you are creating a good or bad name for yourself, your family, your church, and God.

it, our speech should "benefit" listeners (Eph. 4:29). We might greatly enjoy using language, but its primary purpose is to glorify God as we serve our neighbors as ourselves.

For servant speakers, then, there is no place for purely self-serving speech. Speaking at a city council meeting should be just as neighbor-serving as speaking in church, although the verbal and nonverbal language needs to be adapted to each audience.

Speaking Life or Death

The people of Israel spent decades wandering in the wilderness after being freed from Egyptian slavery. Before the Israelites proceeded across the Jordan River, Moses delivered a critically important address. Calling everyone together to renew their covenant with God, Moses said, "I have set before you life and death, blessings and curses. Now choose life, so that you and your children may live" (Deut. 30:19).

Adam chose death by listening to and obeying the serpent—and then deceiving

SERVANT SPEAKING TIP

Strive to become a servant speaker who uses the gift of communication to love God and your neighbor as yourself.

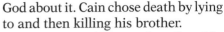

Servant Speaking Tip

Think of speech as a combination of verbal and nonverbal *expression*.

God about it. Cain chose death by lying to and then killing his brother.

Moses wanted his people to flourish, but he feared that when they entered the Promised Land they would forget who had delivered them from Egypt. So Moses warned them to responsibly choose life over death.

Verbal and nonverbal communicating is active decision making. We *do* it. Like other actions, it carries consequences. Speech can lead us to war, persuade us to quit a job, increase our faith, and foster reconciliation. When we lie, we sow seeds of distrust. When we encourage others, we offer hope. The Hebrew term for "word" (*dabar*) means both word and deed.[9]

The concept of speaking life or death reflects the deepest nature of language as relationship-building and relationship-destroying action. "Reckless words pierce like a sword, but the tongue of the wise brings healing," says the writer of Proverbs (12:18). He adds, "The tongue has the power of life and death, and those who love it will eat its fruit" (18:21; see also Pss. 34:12–13; 52:4–5; 1 Pet. 3:10). Matthew says that our words will acquit and condemn us (12:37). James goes so far as to argue that the tongue can corrupt a person and set the "whole course of his life on fire" (3:6).

Few cases are so literal, but an English woman apparently committed suicide because of her neighbors' vicious gossip about her. The coroner said that she was "killed by idle gossip."[10]

Servant Speaking Tip

Select one main speech *purpose* (e.g., informing, persuading, or pleasing) that will direct you to serve your audience responsibly.

Every day we demonstrate the power of saying yes and no to ourselves about our own use of language. Speaking is a series of consequential decisions about *what* to say and *how* and *when* to express it. By saying no to some of our

FINDING AN AUDIENCE-SERVING SPEECH TOPIC

1. list all your major interests and passions—the things you really care about and perhaps know a lot about from your studies, travel, hobbies, work, family life, and more

2. talk to people who represent your likely audience to discover their interests, concerns, and needs

3. determine where 1 and 2 intersect—where your interests connect with the audience members' needs

language (i.e., by not speaking it), we are freer to say yes to God's Word—and then to communicate the Word to others by how we live as well as by what we literally say.

The essence of speaking life is using language responsibly to serve others. Selfish speech eventually gets us into trouble, whereas life-giving speech serves others as we would want to be served. Therefore, the most important question to ask ourselves in preparing a speech is how we intend to serve the audience responsibly as our neighbors. We need to write and rewrite that purpose until we are absolutely sure it is clear and focused on our audience. This book, for instance, is based on the following purpose: to inspire and teach Christians to be skilled, virtuous, and faithful public speakers.

Speaking that currently seems like a chore can eventually make us grateful. Many people are thankful for the gift of public speaking, even though they disliked having to develop the gift during their college years. It gives them self-confidence. For many Christians, learning to speak well has increased

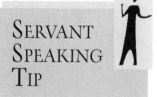

SERVANT SPEAKING TIP

State your specific purpose in only one clear, audience-focused sentence.

BLESSINGS FROM PUBLIC SPEAKING

- delight in serving others through speeches
- gratitude to God for every speech accomplishment
- self-confidence in all speaking
- understanding of and respect for other cultures
- enjoyment of good verbal and nonverbal communication
- discernment of others' attempts to influence you

their faith as they have seen how God speaks life through them.

Regardless of our specific futures, we know that God wants us to speak life by responsibly honoring his name as we serve our audience-neighbors. Moreover, we are blessed when we hold ourselves and one another accountable for doing so.

Conclusion

Servant speaking is a special calling for all of us "response-able" human beings. By speaking life—by faithfully serving our audience-neighbors—we can speak to others as we would like to be spoken to. It is not always easy to discern how to speak responsibly, but the goal is worthy of our calling. After we have done our best, the results are in God's hands.

Augustine learned this when he began attending church services led by St. Ambrose, the bishop of Milan. The pagan Augustine, an unethical rhetorician, went to church not to worship but to pick up a few rhetorical tips from a bishop known as a skilled speaker. Little did Augustine know that God would use Ambrose's gentle, forthright rhetoric to lead Augustine to eternal life in Christ. Ambrose spoke life, and the Spirit gave Augustine eternal life.

Addressing Challenges

Mike Yaconelli, a Christian youth leader and small-town pastor, told of being invited by a friend to address a regional convention of toastmasters—people who meet to practice public speaking. When Yaconelli arrived ten minutes before the event, however, he discovered that the audience members were actually *postmasters*.

Recognizing that he "didn't have much to say about the new bulk mail regulations," Yaconelli decided to speak about something that all people "struggle with—loneliness, insignificance, and meaninglessness." Initially stunned by the last-minute audience change and then shocked by the audience's enthusiastic response to his unprepared remarks, he inadvertently discovered the power of audience-serving communication.[1]

Along the way, Yaconelli faced a challenge that every servant speaker needs to address: potentially destructive fear. This, coupled with two other challenges—excessive ego and undue dependence on technical skills—can sidetrack servant speakers.

Destructive Fear

Holocaust survivor Elie Wiesel is probably the finest public speaker I have heard. His speaking is so engaging, sincere, and convicting that audiences listen carefully and usually respond with standing ovations.

In spite of decades of successful public speaking around the globe, however, Wiesel still suffers from "an accursed companion who never lets go." Wiesel describes his companion: "I suffer

> I appeal to you: Be our [the Jews'] allies. Justify the faith we have in your future. Fight forgetfulness. Reject any attempt to cover up the past . . . and remember: a conscience that does not speak up when injustices are being committed is betraying itself. A mute conscience is a false conscience. Remember some lessons from your past and ours: Words can kill, just as they can heal.
>
> Elie Wiesel, addressing West Germans in 1987, *From the Kingdom of Memory: Reminiscences* (New York: Schocken, 1990), 199

pangs of hell. Butterflies in my stomach. The expression is apt." As he ascends a podium, his body is "seized by trembling" that threatens to paralyze his brain.[2]

Wiesel's destructive companion stays at his side. "I am never sure of myself," he admits. "Will I be able to communicate, to stimulate, to hold the listeners' attention, to logically articulate my ideas? And what if I forget the necessary quotation or the critical point? Once the last sentence has been uttered, I ache to escape."[3]

Fear of public speaking—commonly called speech apprehension—affects even the most gifted speakers. Although fear can be helpful, most of us need to address it head-on so it does not become destructive.

As the account of Adam and Eve's first disobedience shows, fear of interacting with God and other people is natural in a fallen world. After eating the forbidden fruit of the tree of good and evil, the two hide from God. They also put on clothing, becoming the first biblical persons to worry about their public image.

Suffering from broken fellowship with God, we all live with fear and apprehension about relationships. We even worry about whether audiences will accept and like us. Will they gossip about our nervousness or slipups?

NEGATIVE CONSEQUENCES OF EXCESSIVE SPEECH APPREHENSION

- fretting excessively while researching a speech topic

- procrastinating until it is too late to prepare well

- coming across as overly self-conscious when starting delivery

- worrying during delivery about forgetting what to say, losing your place, looking foolish, panicking, or even passing out (which is extremely rare!)

Scripture documents fearful believers. After God appears in the burning bush and commands Moses to tell the Egyptian leaders to liberate his people, Moses anxiously replies, "What if they do not believe me or listen to me?" (Exod. 4:1). So God gives Moses some signs to prove to the Egyptians that God is on his side.

Still anxious, Moses pleads with God, "O Lord, I have never been eloquent, neither in the past nor since you have spoken to your servant. I am slow of speech and tongue" (Exod. 4:10). Moses even tells God that he needs the help of a smooth talker—as if God's authority and commands are not enough help. Before enlisting Aaron to assist Moses, God reminds Moses that he gave him the gift of speech (Exod. 4:11). Later, Moses becomes "powerful in speech" (Acts 7:22). Clearly, Moses underestimated how God could speak through him.

The apostle Paul tells the Corinthians that he came to them in "weakness and fear, and with much trembling" (1 Cor. 2:3). He further admits that, in worldly terms, he is not particularly eloquent or wise when he testifies about God. Peter was so afraid of being associated publicly with Jesus that he denied his Lord three times. Eventually, Peter became an effective, bold preacher, even in the face of ridicule and persecution. Imagine yourself speaking publicly for Jesus in a country hostile to the gospel.

The Benefits of Speech Apprehension

- adrenaline for energetic delivery
- motivation to prepare well
- trust in God even as you work hard

In that context, probably all of us would suffer from speech apprehension, worrying about the consequences of our speech.

Deep down, each of us realizes that we are more or less impostors before an audience. We know things about ourselves that we would not want even a friend to discover. For decades I hid from everyone except close family and friends the fact that I grew up in poverty with an alcoholic father and a schizophrenic mother. It took me years of grappling with my own past, and eventually counseling, before I was able to reveal this even in limited situations. During my life journey, I feared that I was destined to fail. I could hardly face myself, let alone a public audience.

After becoming a teacher, I struggled with apprehension and even panic attacks in front of the very students I was obliged to serve. I knew that even as a professor of communication was a poor communicator! Often I saw that people with less education were more confident and inspiring speakers. Worse yet, I remembered occasions when I had failed miserably as a speaker, such as the time I let down my college classmates with a lackluster section of a class presentation.

To come out of my fear-induced shell, I needed what we all can benefit from: learning how to speak publicly with the help of a beloved community in which we feel cared for, protected, and appreciated for who we are rather than for our accomplishments. A classroom or a speaking club can provide a setting for such safe speaking. Some adults gain confidence by leading children's worship, teaching Sunday school, coaching a team, or telling jokes to friends. I did all of them. To my own surprise, I discovered that public speaking is a lifelong pursuit worthy of patient effort. My apprehension subsided, and I increasingly enjoyed serving audiences. When I failed, I figured out what went wrong and learned from the mistakes.

Regardless of how we get started, we need to admit to God our dependence on him. Job concluded during his time of weakness, "I must speak and find relief; I must open my lips and reply [to God]" (32:20).

Instead of trying to overcome all our speech apprehension, then, we are better off reducing it and then using the remaining apprehension beneficially. God does not expect perfection, only faithfulness. Wiesel's faith in the God of Abraham, Isaac, and Jacob gives him courage to speak forthrightly in a post-Holocaust world. Our faith in Jesus Christ helps us to call on God rather than depend merely on ourselves or other people.

Excessive Ego

The flip side of destructive fear is excessive ego evident in self-righteous and self-centered speech. Normally, this is not much of a problem with newer speakers, but sometimes it affects those who are quick to grow into audience-pleasing speakers.

We all are valuable persons made in God's image. But we ought not think too highly of ourselves, even if we are relatively fearless speakers. Otherwise we might let our egos run loose.

Ego is heady stuff, especially for skilled presenters. When a speaker gets a taste of flattery, he or she becomes susceptible to prideful communication. Augustine warned Christian speakers that it is "difficult and demanding . . . not to be enticed by the bait of praise."[4]

Like fear, destructive human egos appear in the account of the fall. The quest to know good and evil apart from God leads Adam and Eve to view the world egocentrically. They become self-absorbed, dealing with their own shame by blaming others. Adam faults Eve, who blames the serpent for her disobedience.

This ego-excessive condition, known in Hebrew as *pesha*, suggests hard-heart-

SERVANT SPEAKING TIP

Reduce speaking fears by telling your friends stories, including humorous anecdotes.

A REALISTIC VIEW OF HUMAN COMMUNICATION

- confusion: Speakers and listeners are more or less confused.

- self-interest: Egotism seeps into the minds and hearts of all communicators.

- division: Language divides as well as unites people.

edness, pride, and a stubborn refusal to listen to God. Human beings suffering from *pesha* have difficulty responding to God's call to love their neighbors. Instead, they may intentionally deceive audiences, rely on slick delivery to compensate for thin content and even put down others publicly to build up their own image. The biblical view of humans as self-serving communicators may seem excessive, but it is realistic.

Egotistical speakers tend to focus excessively on their own abilities. They place themselves at the center of reality, speaking excessively in the self-indulgent first person. They may even justify deception as a means of persuading supposedly ignorant people to do what is better for them.

As a successful rhetorician, Augustine struggled with ego. Subsequent to his adult conversion, he recalled that he and other rhetoricians had pursued the "empty glory of popularity, ambitious for the applause of the audience." Augustine even confessed that he had tried to distinguish himself as "an orator for a damnable conceited purpose, namely delight in human vanity."[5]

Unrestrained ego infects our speaking with pride. It leads us to see ourselves as great talkers to whom others should listen endlessly. Yet as we grow to enjoy hearing ourselves, our pride interferes with our ability to listen to God and other people. The twentieth-century Trappist monk Thomas Merton wrote in his journal that we humans "interfere with God's work by talking too much about ourselves."[6] John writes in his Gospel, "He who speaks on his own does so to gain honor for himself, but he who works for the honor of the one who sent him is a man of truth" (7:18).

Addressing the effects of ego, the great mathematician and philosopher Blaise Pascal (1623–62) impractically advised, "Do you wish people to believe good in you? Don't speak."[7] He had a point. Most of us probably should spend more time listening to

U2's BONO ON ROCK SINGERS' EGOS

[The] only thing worse than a rock star is a rock star with . . . a Lexus and a swimming pool shaped like his head. . . . [A singer is] someone with a hole in his heart almost as big as the size of his ego. When you need twenty thousand people screaming your name in order to feel good about your day, you know you're a singer.

Harvard University commencement address, 2001, http://www .commencement.harvard.edu/2001/bono_address.html

God and neighbor and less to ourselves. "When words are many, sin is not absent," warns Proverbs (10:19).

A college chaplain seeks to live by this humble rule: Remember that on some issues I might be mistaken. This helps him to remain cautious about his public claims. Used sparingly and honestly, phrases such as "it seems to me," "as best I can determine," "according to my limited research," and "I value your concerns and criticisms" can help us avoid excessive ego without diminishing our authority to speak on topics about which we are informed.

We should speak confidently, even boldly, when appropriate. But we should do so without projecting an air of superiority, as if we are the most important or most knowledgeable people in the world.

A major corporate CEO spoke about the relationship between social justice and management compensation. He explained

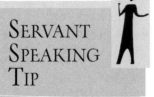

SERVANT SPEAKING TIP

Avoid excessive ego by practicing this rule: Speak only if you are sure you can improve on the silence.

why his company limited executive salaries according to a formula based on a multiple of workers' wages. The CEO began his presentation with an invitation to attendees to prepare their own thoughts for the follow-up Q&A. He said something like this: "I hope we can discuss this issue when I am finished, because I would like to learn from you, and I'm sure you would like to hear from one another as well as from me." This was an inviting, nonegotistical opening without false humility, because he did follow through with open discussion.

An arrogant speaker is egocentrically "consumed by his own lips," says the writer of Ecclesiastes (10:12). Gossip and lies, for instance, usually come back to haunt arrogant fools. Wise speakers have something worthwhile to say; they do not just talk as if the audience cannot wait to hear them.

Servant speaking requires us to discern the line between our own God-given personality and our responsibilities to speak courageously, on the one hand, and our excessively selfish ego, on the other—and then to stay on the humble side of the line. Otherwise, our insatiable egos will tend to bring out the prideful aspects of our personalities. Left unchecked, ego reduces rhetoric to manipulation. Therefore, we servant speakers assess

SIGNS OF EGO-TALK

- unnecessarily fancy words
- moralistic slogans
- self-flattering phrases
- repetitious use of "I" and "me"
- belittling comments about others

our motives as well as our methods. When we speak publicly, are we serving our audience-neighbors or ourselves?

The German theologian Dietrich Bonhoeffer summarized this self-evaluation in the case of reading Scripture publicly: "It will make all the difference between right and wrong reading of Scriptures if I do not identify myself with God but quite simply serve him. Otherwise I will be directing the listeners' attention to myself instead of to the Word."[8]

Overreliance on Technical Skill

In addition to fear and ego, overreliance on technical skill can be a significant challenge. We tend to assume that there are a few skills that, once mastered, will guarantee speaking success.

The best public speaking requires more than mastering skills such as maintaining eye contact with an audience, speaking distinctly, and gesturing. As discussed below, servant speaking also requires good personal character and the wisdom to know when and how to use particular speaking skills.

Rather than doing the hard work necessary to become good speakers, we can fall into the trap of looking for a few simple tricks of the trade. We search for new techniques that will impress audiences. These techniques become magical solutions to our speaking problems—like spoken abracadabras.

Any largely technical approach is too mechanical and inflexible. It assumes that speakers and listeners are machine-like senders and receivers rather than complex moral and spiritual persons. As a result, it reduces speech to delivering static messages effectively rather than serving each audience lovingly.

Overly technical approaches to public speaking have a long history in rhetoric, but today they are most evident in the excessive use of "slideware," such as PowerPoint. Too often speakers assume that a glitzy slide show will be more effective than an oral presentation. Worse yet, some speakers presuppose that graphic illustrations can compensate for superficial content and lifeless delivery. So they invest more time in visual glitz than in crafting and presenting an audience-serving speech.

One result is a growing reaction against the excessive use of slideware. "High-tech heretic" Clifford Stoll says that slideware

COMMON WEAKNESSES IN SLIDEWARE-EXCESSIVE PRESENTATIONS

- lack of solid evidence and careful thought

- limited, hierarchical structure

- fragmented stories and data

- comic-book-like "sales pitch"

- excessive and unoriginal graphics

adapted from Edward Tufte, *The Cognitive Style of PowerPoint* (Cheshire, CT: Edward R. Tufte, 2003)

is "the enemy of a good talk."[9] Although he overstates his case Stoll captures what an increasing number of people feel about slideware: It is overused, poorly used, and misused. The magic of slideware technology might be fading.[10]

Slideware is not always appropriate or effective, but charts and pictures can illustrate a solid speech. Who wants to attend a speech about architecture that does not include photos? Or a chemistry lecture without graphic representation? While even technology-free speech can be poorly done, today too many presenters rely on technology without adequate attention to careful planning, adequate research, good organization, and lively delivery. Slides should *support the speaker,* not *become the message.* Slideware is not a quick fix for a poorly conceived and ineptly delivered speech.

Every new technical skill has the potential to serve God and neighbor. Today, however, our amazement with new computer technologies frequently leads us to adopt new devices too hastily, without attention to serving an audience. Not surprisingly people often resent speakers who waste their time showing hokey slides or merely reading bullet points on a screen. Servant speakers should avoid the temptation to try to beat the world at its own technological game. After all, "fools with tools are still fools."[11]

WHEN TO USE SLIDEWARE IN A SPEECH

- if a large visual is needed to show or demonstrate something

- if handouts are too small, cannot be copied legally, or would require expensive color printing

- when particular sentences, words, or visuals need to be shown repeatedly

- when the audience includes people with hearing difficulties and the venue lacks hearing-assisted technologies

- when copies of the slideware presentation will be made available later to attendees in digital or print formats

We need the wisdom to discern when, where, and why to use particular technical skills. Knowing what to talk about and how best to illustrate a message is more important than being skilled slideware technologists. Just because technology is readily available and easy to use does not mean we should always use it.

Human-created devices are gifts for serving others well, not for avoiding necessary speech research, planning, and practice or for impressing audiences with our technological skill. Using them wisely is essential.

Conclusion

As Yaconelli discovered when he successfully addressed the toastmasters who turned out to be postmasters, we can learn from experience and—with the power of the Spirit—successfully overcome the challenges of public speaking. Practice pays off in the long run, reducing our fear, humbling us as we witness how God speaks through us, and weaning us from excessively technical crutches. Sometimes the path to such self-confidence is rocky, but it can also be inspiring.

Therefore, like Augustine, we face the challenges before us. We prepare well so we can serve our audience-neighbors. Trusting God to speak through us, we begin learning what to say and how to say it.

4

LISTENING WELL

God gives all of us both a curiosity and the capacity to explore his world. In a sense, our lives are journeys of discovery of God, creation, other people, and ourselves. Every day is an opportunity to listen and to learn—and to pass along what we learn that might be helpful to others. Imagine a lonely world where none of us could grow by asking friends, family, neighbors, and colleagues for advice.

Servant speaking benefits from a desire to explore the world and to share our discoveries with one another. We learn primarily by paying attention to the way things are around us, including what we read and hear and our reflections on life experiences. Formal education is only one of the ways we learn.

Biblically speaking, all of this learning is a form of listening, of getting acquainted personally with reality, not just hearing about reality. For example, when we say "I hear you" to someone, we mean more than "I heard your voice." We mean "I understand you." Listening includes every means we use to gain an appreciation for and an understanding of reality.

To speak knowledgeably, we listen *vertically* to God, the ultimate source of wisdom. We also listen *horizontally* to authorities and audiences so that we know in advance what we are speaking about and to whom we will be speaking. Finally, we listen *internally* to ourselves, as well as to others' responses to us, to overcome our weaknesses and to develop our individual servant strengths. All these forms of listening are types of research, where we "re-search" what God already knows.

Vertical Listening—to Wisdom's Source

Rhetoricians historically assumed that studying language would help them to gain truth, be more just, and communicate better. To accomplish these worthy goals, they studied the methods of successful orators past and present. From a Christian perspective, however, the deepest kind of knowing—wisdom—requires knowing God personally (John 14:7; Phil. 3:8), speaking the truth from the heart (Ps. 15:2), and putting the Word into action (James 1:22).[1] Such wisdom is far more than information or knowledge; it is a personal acquaintance with ultimate reality such as who God is, who we are, and why we were created.

This biblical wisdom might seem impractical or inappropriate in some speech situations. After all, what is wisdom on a typical speech topic? Does a religious CEO need to refer to God when addressing shareholders? Should a politician quote Scripture in campaign speeches? What is God's wisdom with regard to an informative speech about tuning up a ten-speed bicycle?

Augustine defined wisdom as personal knowledge of God's "first meanings."[2] He believed that God reveals basic truths that should form the foundation for all human thought and action. Christian philosopher Nicholas Wolterstorff uses the term *control beliefs*—"first" beliefs that should control how we view and act in the world.[3]

All human beings implicitly or explicitly rely on faith-like control beliefs to communicate about important matters. Aristotle, one of the greatest rhetoricians of all time, used the word *pisteis* to refer to the proofs that a speaker employs to support particular positions and to refute others. The root word for *pisteis* means "belief."[4] Aristotle recognized that people's first assumptions tend to be accepted as matters of belief even without voluminous evidence. To have faith in someone, for instance, is to believe (in) him or her, not just to believe what he or she says.

Identifying Speakers' Control Beliefs

- human nature: good, bad, or mixed?
- God: alive, dead, personal, or impersonal?
- purpose of life: glorifying God, serving one's neighbor, serving self, or being indifferent?

The history of Christianity shows how faithful believers adapted control beliefs to ever-changing circumstances—to new forms of music, worship, instruction, and leisure. Although Christian control beliefs are biblically reliable, believers have to relearn them and reexpress them for each generation. As writer Walker Percy puts it, Christian language tends to "wear out and get stored in the attic." Christians must "renew language" in order to "sing a new song."[5] Even cherished terms such as *salvation, holiness,* and *peace* need to be renewed or they will grow stale and meaningless. Christian speakers have to be wise enough to reach deeper than superficial clichés, even if they do not always express their control beliefs explicitly to non-Christian audiences.

Therefore, when appropriate and possible, we should anchor our speech ideas in biblical control beliefs. A CEO's statement on how business can best serve employees and customers should be "controlled" by his or her faith. Similarly, a store manager might articulate how retail workers can truly serve customers as neighbors. A student might address leisure, exercise, and stewardship as the contexts for why it is important to tune up a bicycle. Sometimes Christians and non-Christians will use identical language, but even then the motivation of Christian speakers might be different. A Christian store manager might give employees a motivational talk to encourage them to serve customers well, not just to make a profit for the company.

When we move from our control beliefs to legitimate areas of Christian disagreement, we can either humbly admit ambiguity or pretend we have achieved perfect wisdom. Speakers who fall into the latter trap tend to "preachify"—to moralize tirelessly at others. Some egotistical preachifiers seem to believe that even

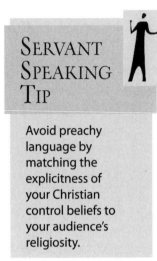

SERVANT SPEAKING TIP

Avoid preachy language by matching the explicitness of your Christian control beliefs to your audience's religiosity.

the most complex, non-control-belief issue is black and white, with no middle ground.

Servant speakers sometimes speak openly about their control beliefs, but they recognize that not everyone will agree even with their most cherished assumptions. They realize that speaking arrogantly is generally counterproductive as well as preachy. And they avoid equating their personal attitudes with control beliefs. Having "feelings" about something is not the same as being wise. We all have impressions and opinions that are not anchored in reality. These include stereotypes, unsubstantiated rumors, racial and ethnic prejudices, and probably some of our mistaken notions about how to apply Scripture to culture.

A servant speaker *seeks* to know God's wisdom without pretending to *be* God. The Danish church gadfly Søren Kierkegaard (1813–53) said that "God bestowed the gift of speech upon humanity out of love, so making it possible for all to gain a real understanding of the highest—oh, with what sorrow must God look down on the result!"[6] We gain an understanding of all things by listening to God and then to authorities and audiences.

Horizontal Listening—to Authorities and Audiences

Preparing a speech requires horizontal listening to two categories of people: (1) *authorities* who are knowledgeable about the speech topic and (2) people who represent the likely *audience*. Listening to authorities helps us to know what we are talking about so that the content of a speech is not merely our own unsupported opinions. Listening to those who represent our likely audience helps us adapt the content and the style of a speech to the people we aim to serve. Both types of listening are called research, which means re-searching what others already know so that we can become knowledgeable as well.

To ensure that we know our topic and our audience well, we conduct both primary and secondary research. Although on-the-spot (impromptu) speaking does not provide the time for preparatory research, nearly all other speeches for any of the three major purposes—informing, pleasing, and persuading—require such research.

Primary Research

Primary research is firsthand listening that takes us directly to the authorities and audience. For example, if we are preparing an informational speech for an adult Sunday school class on the topic of the religious beliefs of the signers of the Declaration of Independence, we should listen to what the signers themselves said about their faith. We would probably have to search for copies of their own speeches and writings—what they themselves said about their religious convictions. If we relied only on what other writer-researchers said about the founders' faith, unless we are absolutely certain about the accuracy of these authorities' research, we might pass along to our audience incomplete or even incorrect information.

Similarly, we should listen to likely members of our Sunday school audience. We should ask them what they already know or believe about the topic—and perhaps why they believe it and where they learned it. We would want to discover, if possible, the sources they listen to regarding the topic, such as particular authors or broadcast personalities who have shaped their views on the topic.

Sometimes one of the most important primary sources is ourselves. Often our life experiences represent an important source of primary information. Of course, our knowledge of a topic might not be accurate or representative of what others know and believe. Nevertheless, we all have hobbies, work and life experiences, and personal areas of study that make us valuable sources if not expert authorities. Moreover, we can imagine ourselves as members of some audiences—such as our own

experience as a member of the Sunday school class we will ad
dress. So we should listen to ourselves to learn from our pas
and present experiences.

Secondary Research

Nearly every good speech is based on secondary research o
what authorities have concluded about the topic and likely au
dience. Secondary sources have already interpreted primary
sources. For example, historians previously examined the
speeches and writings of many of the signers of the Declara
tion of Independence, including those signers' views of religion
So have many researchers who would not consider themselve
professional historians, such as theologians, attorneys, and re
ligious activists.

Almost every imaginable speech topic has already been inves
tigated by researchers who have examined at least some primary
sources. This is why it is essential to consult online research
databases while preparing a speech. Some secondary sources
might be suspect because they represent a special interest group
or the researchers used shoddy research methods such as unrep
resentative survey questionnaires or selective primary sources
But we still need to consult secondary sources to come to our
own knowledgeable conclusions.

A primary source for one speech might be secondary for a dif
ferent topic or audience. If we are giv
ing a speech about delivering speeches
this book would be a secondary source
because it is based primarily on my
views of what people such as Augus
tine have written on the topic. But i
we are preparing a presentation on
my views of the historic art of public
speaking, this book could serve as a pri
mary source.

Generally speaking, there are two
kinds of secondary sources—those avail
able in popular and academic media
Popular sources include radio and TV
program interviews, newspaper and

SERVANT
SPEAKING
TIP

Search scholarly
journals to find
supporting
information
from respected
authorities.

magazine articles, and mass-market books sold in most bookstores and available in neighborhood libraries. Academic sources are available almost exclusively in scholarly journals and books that are read primarily by professors and other researchers.

Most academic publications are specialized for particular research disciplines, such as psychology, chemistry, economics, and history. The public can gain access to them at college and university libraries or in some cases via the Internet. A common problem occurs when public speakers rely only on popular sources without consulting the more expert academic sources. For instance, much of the popular writing and speaking about the religious convictions of the signers of the Declaration of Independence ignores the more scholarly historical research and selectively quotes only a few of the signers. Popular speakers on this subject frequently pick and choose primary sources in order to confirm their preexisting conclusions. They know how to please their audiences but fail to serve them well with unbiased presentations.

Researching for Mind and Heart

Often the best speeches appeal logically to audience members' minds (*logos*), emotionally to their hearts (*pathos*), or to both. Therefore, we need to make sure we have listened adequately to authorities and representatives of the likely audience. If we do not have a clear sense of what will effectively teach, please, or move our audience, we have not conducted adequate research.

At a persuasive lecture meant to defend belief in God, the speaker used quotations from great Western philosophers and theologians. Clearly, he knew the views of important authorities on the topic, but he mistakenly offered only one logical argument after another in support of the thesis that God exists. He so thoroughly relied on famous minds and propositional logic (e.g., If there is a universe, there must be a maker of that universe.) that there was little room left for basing belief on a heartfelt sense that God exists (e.g., Just as I can love others, I feel loved by them and by a personal Creator God.). Since faith comes from the heart as well as the mind, the speaker probably needed more *pathos*.

> **SERVANT SPEAKING TIP**
>
> Listen well to the minds and hearts of your likely audience members to learn how *they* think and feel about the topic.

On the other hand, if we focus ou research too much on *pathos*—on the emotional appeals that will move our au dience—we risk being perceived by ou audience as passionately ill informed For instance, some people praise or con demn popular Christian music withou examining it, exploring the industry tha produces and distributes it, or listenin, to those who find the music meaningfu or meaningless. In most circumstances we need to demonstrate to our audience neighbors that we have done our researcl adequately, that we are informed as wel as passionate about our topic.

Listening enables us to become "all things to all people" b understanding and even empathizing with our audience-neigh bors. As we get to know the likely audience's makeup—such a demographics, values, and assumptions—we can form an audi ence profile that equips us to imagine whom we are serving.

Servant speakers do not compromise their control beliefs o pander to an audience, but they do adapt their messages to thei audience members by listening to them or to people like them

> **SERVANT SPEAKING TIP**
>
> Listen to other speakers to learn how they use primary and secondary research, including personal anecdotes and published sources.

Active, engaged listening—along witl any needed follow-up interaction—i the primary way we intentionally lear about others, including how we cai serve them as audience-neighbors.

Horizontal listening helps us t learn when and how to express contro beliefs in tune with specific audiences We adjust our level of religious explicit ness to each audience. A friend puts i this way: "To a general audience, I speal as a human being. With other believers I talk as a Christian. With those whe share my Roman Catholic faith, I ente the discussion as a Catholic. But in eacl case, the basic thrust of my words is ii tune with my faith."

Before he addressed the Greek philosophers at the Areopagus on Mars Hill, Paul observed Athenians, engaged them in conversations, and studied their art. Paul became "greatly distressed to see that the city was full of idols" (Acts 17:16). But his listening paid off. In fact, having heard about his speeches, the philosophers invited Paul to speak to them (Acts 17:19).

In the synagogue at Antioch, Paul the Jew referred to God's chosen people. As a former persecutor of Christians, he knew this audience firsthand! Paul recognized that he needed to translate his Christian control beliefs into audience-connecting speeches (Acts 13). Paul used both *pathos* and *logos* appropriately for various audiences, appealing to hearts and minds, to the whole person.

Internal Listening—to Our Naked Selves

In his *Confessions,* Augustine describes his conversion in the context of his work as a rhetorician. He says that he stood naked before himself, becoming his own audience.[7] Augustine saw his pride and recalled his deceptiveness. From then on, he recognized that he needed to be honest about himself to others. Realizing that God knew him personally, Augustine had no place left to hide. Once a rhetorician who taught others how to lie effectively, he now thanked God for "delivering" his tongue.[8]

Learning to be a servant speaker includes lifelong self-evaluation. For many of us, this is painful. We do not want to consider how others and God might view us. We prefer to hide behind our fragile self-images, hoping that audience-neighbors will never see us as we really are.

Yet listening to ourselves is critically important for loving others *as ourselves*. We need to discover our speaking strengths and weaknesses, including the topics that interest us and that match our rhetorical gifts.

Self-listening, sometimes called intrapersonal communication, requires stripping away layers of self-denial and dialoguing with ourselves. We then become naked to ourselves—to our misdirected desires, bad habits, and recurrent weaknesses, as well as to our insufficient knowledge and undeveloped skills. We might discover that we procrastinate before speeches, do research superficially, use sources sloppily, or practice delivery

SERVANT
SPEAKING
TIP

Record in a journal what you learn about yourself after each speech, including comments from attendees and official evaluators. Review your entries in preparation for later speeches.

inadequately. Augustine warned that people who fail to listen to themselves will discover that others do not listen to them![9]

We might discern that we have special speaking gifts that can be developed. Few highly effective adult speakers knew by high school or early college that God had granted them gifts such as verbal fluency, bodily expressiveness, or argumentational abilities.

Because we deceive ourselves about ourselves, we also need to examine ourselves in the light of how others see us. Reviewing others' responses to our speeches can be enormously helpful.

When we are evaluated, most of us tend initially to accept praise and to reject criticism. We do not want to face our weaknesses. As a result, we sometimes carry the same weaknesses from speech to speech without learning and improving.

Listening openly to ourselves, including how others respond to us, enables us to learn from our successes and failures. Servant speaking is a lifetime journey of learning how to better serve audience-neighbors.

Conclusion

Listening well helps us to speak well. We learn wisdom primarily by dwelling in a community that worships the source of all wisdom and studies his Word and world. Unless we know God and anchor our control beliefs in his Word, our basic assumptions about ultimate reality could lead us and others astray.

We learn about topics and audiences by listening to primary and secondary sources. We might not agree fully with secular experts, but we can gain information and knowledge from them.

Finally, we learn by listening to ourselves in relationship with God and others. It is so easy for us to deceive ourselves, to think we are better or worse speakers than we really are or that we are adequately or inadequately prepared to speak on a particular topic to a specific audience.

Vertical, horizontal, and internal listening can help us to love our audience-neighbors as ourselves—to be all things to all people. Without such listening, we are less likely to serve others.

As Augustine said, all truth is God's truth, regardless of where we discover it. Stretching to listen beyond our existing knowledge, we will all come face-to-face with a Creator God who is sustaining an incredibly complex, interesting, and surprising world. No matter where and when we attend to reality, if we persevere with open hearts and minds, we will discover an authoritative Creator who is already listening and speaking to us—so might those who listen to us, if we are good listeners too.

5

CRAFTING ARTFULLY

The prophet Jeremiah showed the Judeans a clay pot and told them that it represented them. Then he smashed it to pieces to illustrate how God might deal with their disobedience (chap. 19). His goal was to draw attention to God's Word, not to the illustration itself. Jeremiah's artful visualization reinforced his important message long before the invention of PowerPoint.

Language and visual image have always worked together, if only because audiences usually see the speakers. Jeremiah could have used only spoken words, but his multimedia demonstration helped the Judeans see, hear, and perhaps even smell God's displeasure as the dust rose from the ground. Jeremiah used his body as well as his voice to make his point.

Even with today's presentation technologies, a servant speaker's main medium is still the body, including the face, voice, and arms. They help a speaker express ideas artfully as well as effectively.

Delivered with the body, a well-crafted speech still should satisfy at least three artistic standards: thematic unity, expressiveness, and situational fit. Moreover, it pleasingly employs the art of illustrative storytelling.

Thematic Unity

Well-crafted speeches are like good jazz music—variations on a rich theme. They relate all content and delivery to one major thesis. What if Martin Luther King Jr. had said, "I've got some dreams" instead of "I have a dream"? King's skill at building speeches on one important point—his ability to create thematic unity—enhanced his rhetorical effectiveness.

Listeners deserve to know the main point of any presentation. Therefore, we speakers ought to ask ourselves, What's the principal point of my speech? That point is the speech's main idea or thesis.

Simple Logic

One way to gain thematic unity is through simple logic—developing a thesis with one or more logically supporting subpoints that will connect with the audience.

Here is a thesis: Thematically unified speeches serve audiences better than thematically disjointed speeches. Here are three logical subpoints about how thematic unity serves audiences: (1) by helping audience-neighbors understand the thesis, (2) by helping listeners remember the speech, and (3) by making the main point of the speech more artistically pleasing for the audience.

I learned about the importance of simple logic during a de-

cade of speaking to parents about the impact of media on children. Because most parents are busy, I needed a clear and logically compelling thesis with no more than two or three easily remembered, practical subpoints. I settled on this thesis: Parents can successfully teach their children media discernment. My two logical subpoints were: (1) Parents should be involved in nonmedia activities with their children to build mutually trusting relationships, and (2) parents should discuss media products with their children. I called

EXPRESS A THESIS SPECIFICALLY

- an overly general thesis: This speech is about TV, parents, and children.

- an adequately specific thesis: Teach your children media discernment by building strong relationships and discussing TV with them.

hese two points *relationship* and *discussion*, respectively (the R&D of building children's media discernment).

To motivate parents to put these principles into action, I illustrated them with stories from my family and friends' families. The stories emotionally conveyed the benefits of relational media discernment for deeper, richer family life. They developed the necessary *pathos* for my logically organized speeches.

Dialectical Logic

Another approach to unity is dialectical logic—developing both the pros and the cons of a thesis to show that the pros are more convincing than the cons.

Dialectic means back and forth, yes versus no, or thesis-antithesis. From a Christian perspective, dialectic is sometimes the most helpful way of integrating control beliefs into presentations, since we know that God created the world "very good," but the same world is now deeply fractured under the weight of sin. Few things are totally good or totally evil (only God is completely good). All arguments have weaknesses and contrary arguments. We know we all are broken individuals, simultaneously saints and sinners, as Martin Luther put it.

One practical advantage to dialectical over simple logic is that the former requires a speaker to address an audience's likely opposition (the cons) to a thesis. Neither of the two subpoints in the earlier paragraph addresses the cons of R&D for some parents, such as a single-parent family in which the working father or mother with custody does not have much relational time to spend with the children.

Every well-researched speech requires a speaker to research opposing theses or at least contrary information, since the audience might hold such ideas and information. Dialectical logic, however, requires a speaker to address opposing ideas and information head-on. For example, a persuasive speech about the long-term stewardship benefits of buying a gas-electric hybrid car probably should address potential drawbacks, such as a higher purchase price as well as more expensive insurance and repair costs.

Problem-Solution Logic

A third way of achieving unity is through problem-solution logic—stating a problem that an audience likely faces and then showing how the thesis offers a reasonable solution to that problem.

Here is a possible problem: How can a person find time for daily prayer? Surveys have shown that most Christians desire to pray more but are strapped for time. They are already emotionally predisposed to pray, perhaps even feeling guilty, but they do not know how to find the time without sacrificing needed sleep or desired career advancement. The answer usually has to do with reducing

ELEMENTS OF AN AUDIENCE-SERVING INTRODUCTION

- engage your audience with an interesting story, fact, or idea

- clarify your purpose

- state your thesis in one clear sentence

- preview briefly your main points

- establish your servant *ethos*

- transition to the body of the speech

some of the personal time dedicated to less-important, less-refreshing leisure, such as pointless Internet or TV channel surfing.

Elements of a Unified Speech

Regardless of how we mix and match simple, dialectical, and problem-solution logic in a speech, we still need to clarify the resulting unity for the audience. In short, we need to tell the audience what we intend to say, then say it, and finally remind the audience what we just said. These three elements are called the introduction, body, and conclusion of a speech.

The best way of quickly engaging an audience in an introduction is with a story that illustrates the main point of the speech. Often the most engaging story is personal, such as the time we did something that illustrates our thesis.

When did we realize that our prayer life suffered because we were overly busy? How did we respond to that realization? What did we learn from others about the problem or the solutions? By asking ourselves such questions, we might recall stories that connect with audience members' own similar experiences.

During the body of a speech, a servant speaker states subpoints, explains supporting evidence derived from listening to sources, uses illustrative stories, and addresses possible audience objections. Whether they are logical or emotional, clear transitions help the audience follow the verbal flow from point to point. Sometimes it helps to restate the thesis with each new subpoint and before each new transition.

Probably the most frequently used type of transition for organizing the body of the speech is numbered subpoints (first, second, third, etc.). A four-part persuasive speech on losing weight could include the following two of three sequential subpoints as transitions: The first way to shed a few pounds is to say no to most desserts. The second way to shed a few pounds is to check the calorie count on packaged food labels and stay within your set range. These kinds of transitions work well to help listeners follow the speech, but they are not very creative and do not help the audience remember the subpoints very well.

A second approach is to use one or more visual metaphors for subpoints, preferably related directly to the speech topic. Such metaphors might include a painting, a drawing, a photograph, or an artifact. A four-leaf clover might work, with each of the leaves representing one subpoint. Slideware could show each of the leaves as they are added to the clover, or each of the leaves coming off the clover as the plant "slims down." The title might be "How to Have More Luck Losing Weight," since four-leaf clovers are associated with good luck.

A third way of building memorable transitions into a speech is to use acronym-based subpoints that can be reduced to one memorable keyword: SLIM down by *s*aying no to desserts, *l*ooking up calorie counts on labels, *i*ncreasing water intake, and *m*oving around to burn off excess fat.

Audiences find unity pleasing as well as helpful. A speech does not have to be simplistic to be well unified. Simple, dialectical, and problem-solution logic can serve as helpful approaches depending on the situation. In nearly every case, however, a speech should be easy to follow with an engaging introduction, point-to-point transitions, and a conclusion that restates the thesis and clarifies what the speaker would like the audience to know, believe, or do.

Expressiveness

Audiences rightly dislike lifeless speeches. Some people arrive early at speeches to get a seat by the door so they can escape unobtrusively if the presentation is uninteresting. They expect to be disappointed.

Communicating well requires expressiveness—nonverbal and verbal delivery that appropriately engages audience-neighbors. A

Major Body "Media"

- gesturing with arms and hands
- connecting with eyes directed to listeners
- moving with legs and feet
- affirming with smiles

speech is a performance, not merely a manuscript, an outline, or slides. Nor is a speech just a reading, although a speaker appropriately might recite a prepared manuscript in some circumstances. Good speeches are orally and visually expressive performances by which a speaker serves an audience with mind, heart, and body.

No two speakers are likely to use their body in precisely the same ways, nor should they try to do so. Just as there are many musical styles, there are many delivery styles. Orators used to talk about grand, intermediate, and plain styles, but even such distinctions barely began to address the incredible variety of people and communicative gifts. Given the fact that we differ in terms of large and small motor coordination, disabilities, body height, personality, and more, we need to identify some of the major body "media" and then develop our own styles that work well for who we are and how we are able to express ourselves.

Speeches briefly place a privileged speaker before an expectant audience. Just by showing up, audience members say, "Let's give our time and attention to this speaker." Moreover, audience members normally want to respond with warm applause and sincere words of thanks. They hope that the speaker will engage them successfully. In short, they want a fully expressive performance, not just a boring reading or a lifeless delivery.

If a person is unable to employ some nonverbal means because of injury or genetic disability, he or she should concentrate on those that are available. No matter which parts of the body are used, a speaker gives birth to a speech while delivering it. The speech becomes a living performance, a one-time event that can never be perfectly repeated. A servant speaker carefully works on bodily delivery as well as the message because both contribute to the success or failure of a speech performance.

Nonverbal Expressiveness

Artful speakers use nonverbal expression, including arm-hand gestures, smiles, and eye contact. They "embody" the meaning of the words not just by speaking them but by reinforcing them visually. Many people do this well in conversation but then stiffen up when speaking publicly.

The twentieth-century American rhetorician Kenneth Burke says that when we humans speak in person we naturally use our bodies. He suggests that "beneath the dance of words" always lies a "dance of bodies."[1] The dance metaphor might seem far-fetched, but it appropriately captures the thrust of nonverbal expression.

Augustine offered a wonderful metaphor for nonverbal expressiveness based on Psalm 149. He encouraged Christians to "praise the Lord" with their "whole selves," not just their voices.[2] In the same way, servant speakers should use their physical presence to connect with audience-neighbors. "The soul speaks in the movements of the body," St. Ambrose (340–397) told young priests.[3]

> **SERVANT SPEAKING TIP**
>
> Use whatever nonverbal means are available and fitting—such as arms, hands, and eyes—to express yourself.

Facial expressiveness is vital. In the Old Testament, God rarely shows his face to people because it is so personal and because God is so holy. But Jacob gets to see God in person. The incredible event changed how he perceived people too. Upon being received in friendship by his brother Esau, Jacob declares, "For to see your face is like seeing the face of God, now that you have received me favorably" (Gen. 33:10).

A friendly countenance is a nonverbal invitation to relationship. Warm facial expressions suggest favoritism, which literally means "lifting up" our faces to one another. An audience wants to see, not just hear, a speaker's favor.

Cicero argued that "all depends on countenance; and even in that the eyes bear sovereign sway."[4] From the moment a speaker enters the room, the audience begins tentatively "reading" the speaker's face. Once the speaker begins, nonverbal expression can suggest meanings either in tune with or in contrast to the intended meaning of the speech. If the speaker fails to look at the audience, he or she implicitly conveys shyness or indifference. Orators who maintain regular eye contact and smile appropriately thereby express a caring attitude.

Verbal Expressiveness

Verbal (or vocal) expressiveness is so important that most audiences quickly tune out a monotonic speaker. Our voices are like musical instruments; each one has its own normal frequency range and power, but every voice has expressive potential when used skillfully.

SERVANT SPEAKING TIP

Enhance your verbal expressiveness by varying your verbal (1) pace, (2) loudness, and (3) frequency range.

Normally, vocal pacing should be slower at the beginning of a speech and faster toward the conclusion, with variations along the way for story action. Loudness should support the importance of the point being made; the more significant the point, the more a speaker should emphasize it loudly. Frequency should match emotions, such as a higher-pitched delivery to express astonishment.

Martin Luther King Jr. honed his delivery, trying out various vocal emphases and cadences as he traveled from church to church. Those who lived through the Civil Rights era still recall his booming and quivering voice as well as his upright posture and active arms and hands. He was a verbal artist whose power derived not just from the content of his speeches but also from the ways he passionately vocalized his ideas.

SERVANT SPEAKING TIP

Replace verbal fillers with silence, which respectfully gives the audience a chance to think. It also gives you more time to recall or plan your next point, renew eye contact, and survey audience reactions.

One of the worst types of inexpressiveness is verbal fillers, such as *um, ah, ya'know, like, kinda, so, sorta, just,* and sometimes *and*. The most common ones, *um* and *ah*, are nearly always meaningless distractions. Each one becomes a vocal hiccup, detracting from the significance of the adjacent phrases and creating choppy delivery, inarticulateness, and noisy nonsense.

AUGUSTINE'S WORDPLAY— PLEASING OR SILLY?

- "Faith must *hold* what it cannot yet *behold*."
- "The fisherman's *scope* is the rhetorician's *hope*." (about St. Peter)
- "The damage is not done *by militia-ness* but by *maliciousness*." (about the military profession not being inherently evil)

Garry Wills, *Saint Augustine* (New York: Viking, 1999), 70

Consider what this public prayer would sound like: "Like, you know, Lord, we're just kinda grateful." Now contrast it with this direct, meaningful prayer: "Lord, we are grateful."

Augustine believed that speakers should use any appropriate verbal and nonverbal means to engage audiences. He encouraged Christian teachers and preachers to employ catchy witticisms. Augustine's goal was not foremost to amuse but to draw an audience into his presentations. Even when speaking in a "plain style," wrote Augustine, "believers should take steps to be heard not only with understanding but with pleasure and assent."[5]

Nonverbal and verbal expressions are critically important for connecting with audiences. Our bodies and voices are God-given means of expression. But we also have to express ourselves fittingly in each situation.

Situational Fit

Reminiscent of Augustine, Blaise Pascal wrote that a speaker should help others to listen "without pain and with pleasure." He encouraged speakers to focus on the "simple and natural, and not to magnify that which is little, or belittle that which is great." Pascal concluded that a speech should be "suitable."[6] In other words, a servant speaker matches content and delivery to each situation: the audience, the event, and the available time.

Audience Fit

Not all topics, illustrations, gestures, and vocal styles fit all audiences. What is fitting for a Sunday congregation might not be appropriate for an office presentation or a pregame rally for fans. What is verbally and nonverbally proper for a high school class might not fit a presidential address to the United Nations.

A well-known radio personality addressed an education-oriented audience made up largely of Christians. The host mistakenly assumed that the audience would want to hear about the personal lives of some celebrity artists, including their sexual adventures. Along the way he acted like a standup comic, even laughing self-admiringly at his off-color jokes. He failed to match his expressiveness and the content of his speech to the audience.

SERVANT SPEAKING TIP

Determine if a word or phrase is merely a verbal filler by singing the complete sentence. Verbal fillers awkwardly interfere with the flow of the lyrics.

QUESTIONS TO ASK FOR AUDIENCE FIT

- What are the audience members' existing feelings about the topic?

- What are their existing moral or ethical convictions?

- Are they likely to be sensitive to particular control beliefs?

- What kind of verbal expressiveness would be proper?

Event Fit

Speeches also need to fit a specific event (or occasion) as it unfolds. When a speaker arrives at a venue, he or she needs to pay attention to what people are hearing and seeing. Perhaps there is a pre-speech meal with invited guests—a great time to ask questions and to get to know the audience better. There might be an event program to review with the host.

Some early rhetoricians scorned orators who planned and rehearsed their speeches so painstakingly that there was no room left for adapting the content and delivery to the unfolding occasion. Part of their concern was probably rivalry between those who preferred verbal precision and those who were comfortable being more spontaneous, like contemporary disagreements between pastors who prefer to read carefully crafted sermon manuscripts and those who believe they connect better with a congregation by being open to new thoughts and responding expressively to unpredictable congregational reactions during delivery.

Instructors understand the need for some last-minute classroom fit because every lecture and each discussion is a special occurrence on one day and at one time. A college professor who teaches two sections of the same course will almost always encounter different student reactions to the same unfolding lecture or discussion questions. Therefore, master teachers learn to plan well while still being open to classroom improvisation. They especially watch students' facial reactions and pause regularly for follow-up discussion.

Speeches are living events until concluded. Speaking *by* heart does not mean merely memorizing a manuscript; it also requires speaking *from* the heart by connecting with a particular audience on a particular occasion. When a speaker truly connects, he or she gains presence—the audience's sense that the speaker is there just for them and worthy of their attention.

The type of speech that most demands last-minute fit is impromptu speaking—speaking on the spur of the moment with little time for preparation. Sometimes people call this speaking off-the-cuff, which refers to an old practice of jotting notes on one's sleeve instead of writing them on an available napkin or piece of paper.

Impromptu speakers have to size up a situation quickly, offering fitting words and expressiveness in tune with the purpose of the unplanned address. Why are we being asked to speak, or why do we feel called to speak up? To offer greetings? To introduce a topic or person? To encourage or to thank others? To confirm what others have said or to express a contrary opinion?

In any case, an impromptu speaker usually serves an audience by offering a clear, simple thesis and concrete examples and illustrations from personal experience, all within the purpose for the occasion. Saying too much risks disorganization. Saying too little risks unimportance.

A church took a congregational vote to offer a position to one of two potential pastors. After the tallying was complete, the counters reported that the two candidates had received an equal number of votes. Everyone was stunned. Elders said there was nothing in the congregation's bylaws about this anomaly. An elderly, founding member of the congregation stood up and gave an impromptu speech of encouragement, concluding that everyone should trust in God and take another vote. He prayed, the congregation revoted, and one candidate gained a majority. A wise member of the church saved the day with fitting words.

Speeches normally should combine careful preparation with sensitive adjustments during delivery. This combination of planning and intra-speech refitting is a strong argument for learning extemporaneous speaking—fairly spontaneous delivery based on a carefully crafted sentence outline and usually including some memorized sections, such as an introduction, transitions, subpoint sentences, short quotations, sources, and conclusion.

Extemporaneous speaking combines well-researched, solidly organized content with flexibly expressive delivery. Some accomplished extemporaneous speakers write out the text of a speech, reread it many times until they know much of it by heart, and then deliver the speech creatively without the manuscript.

Most extemporaneous speakers prepare for delivery with the help of an extended sentence outline. They review the outline repeatedly to memorize the sequence along with key phrases and sources.

SERVANT SPEAKING TIP

Make the transition from reading a manuscript to speaking extemporaneously by telling illustrative stories without notes to a group of friends.

Servant Speaking Tip

Always verify in advance the time allocated for your speech and Q&A, rehearse the timing, and stay on schedule during the speech.

A week or so before the speech, they start delivering it to themselves without notes, glancing at the outline for help as needed. Eventually, they practice it with colleagues, friends, or family.

Available Time

Regardless of whether we use a manuscript or an outline, we need to respect our audience by staying within the allotted time for our speech. Shorter speeches are rarely disasters if they are researched and delivered well, but excessively long speeches can frustrate and bore audiences.

Servant speakers should practice timing, estimating how long each part of a speech should take. If we get behind schedule during delivery, we should edit the outline delivery on the fly. Usually the easiest adjustments are made to the lengths of illustrative stories, which can be elaborated on or truncated with minimal loss of speech content.

Illustrative Storytelling

Learning how to tell a fitting story well is essential for servant speaking. For one thing, stories are the most engaging mode of human communication. For another, stories are so roomy that they can be adapted to many purposes by emphasizing various characters, actions, and themes. Finally, stories offer wonderful possibilities for expressive verbal and nonverbal delivery.

Most storytelling emerges naturally from everyday events. A eulogist recalls an episode from a deceased person's life. Dinner guests swap anecdotes about raising children. College roommates laugh together about professors' absentmindedness (such as one who mistakenly gave the same lecture to a class two days in a row).

A successful filmmaker judges whether a story could be a good screenplay by seeing how well listeners respond to a personal telling of the tale. He likes to interrupt his own storytelling by excusing himself to make a phone call. When he returns, he waits to see if his companions ask him to finish the story. If so, the tale might make a good script. If not, either the story or his telling of it is deficient.

Probably the chief purpose of storytelling in a speech is to illustrate a point pleasingly. Nearly every engaging speech has at least two illustrative stories. Relevant stories help listeners relate personally to and understand a speaker's ideas.

One way to uncover stories is by keeping a file of interesting ones appearing in newspapers, magazines, and books. Another way is by paying attention to everyday conversations and events. By collecting stories and sharing them with friends, we discover which ones seem to serve particular listeners and occasions well. The result is a repertoire from which we can select relevant stories for each speech.

The old expression that life is stranger than fiction is somewhat true. Each of our lives is a series of events, some of which are interesting or telling enough to delight, persuade, or teach others. We frequently tell such stories, like parables, but forget to include appropriate ones in speeches.

ELEMENTS OF A WELL-TOLD STORY

- setting: describe vividly where and when it takes place

- characters: paint visual images with your words and body to illustrate how people look and act

- motivation: explain what the characters are trying to accomplish or overcome

- timing: keep the story moving, delivering key lines at the right places and concluding the story before it wears thin or dominates the entire speech

- relevance: make sure the story is relevant to the point of the speech

Those of us who grew up in storytelling families are inclined to carry on the practice at mealtimes, during special events such as reunions, weddings, and funerals, and amid everyday conversation. But all of us need to remind ourselves that well-crafted speeches are rarely just information. Audiences want to be engaged in a speech, often with *pathos*. Even those of us who are not practiced storytellers tend to be story listeners. We desire helpful, interesting, relevant stories that meaningfully capture life.

Preparing and delivering well-crafted speeches require fluent storytelling. When we stand before an audience, we are not only preparing to tell a few stories about a topic but also participating with the audience in giving birth to a speaking event. Later, someone will ask others about the speech: "How was it?" Whether that person can respond with a story we told is one good indicator of how well we are crafting speeches.

Conclusion

Becoming an artful servant speaker is a lifelong journey. There are no easily learned techniques that fit all situations. Mistakes are common. But we do not need to aim for perfection. We only need to learn and practice as best we can the essentials of well-crafted, audience-serving speeches.

The real fun of servant speaking is learning by crafting. A servant speaker is like a gardener who discovers season after season how best to care for different types of topics and audiences in changing conditions.

Just as a plant needs light, water, and soil, a speech needs particular elements to flourish. Unity gives a speech coherence. Expressive verbal and nonverbal delivery engages the audience. Situational fit tunes the performance to the audience, event, and available time. Storytelling enlivens and illustrates a speech. Jeremiah demonstrated all of this during a persuasive speech that included smashing a clay pot at the feet of the Judeans, thereby telling a story about their own destruction if they did not change their ways.

6

SPEAKING TRUTHFULLY

A graduating high school student was silenced during his commencement address. According to a news report, more than a thousand attendees watched as officials disconnected the microphone when he began describing the school as a "prison system." The undelivered section of the speech reportedly would have called the high school a "foul institution" and a "horribly irresponsible and depraved place."[1]

School officials, parents, and other graduates disagreed over censorship. Some parents said he should have been allowed to finish. Others justified censorship, arguing that the student was supposed to present the views of most seniors, not his own opinions.

Another issue was whether the inner-city school actually operated like a prison. Was the speaker being truthful? If so, should he have been silenced?

Throughout history, secular and religious rhetoricians usually emphasized the importance of truthful speech. Augustine believed that one should always tell the truth, even though some lies are greater sins than others, with lies about Christian doctrine being the worst offenses.[2]

When some rhetoricians embraced deceptive practices, Christians tended to take them to task. Blaise Pascal warned that false eloquence persuades with sweetness rather than with authority.[3] Søren Kierkegaard wished "goodnight" to such ear-tickling eloquence.[4]

A servant speaker accepts responsibility for using words and images truthfully. Four aspects of truthful speech are God-talk, doubt-talk, honest-talk, and straight-talk.

God-Talk—Expressing God's Revealed Wisdom

In court, we ask witnesses to raise their right hand and to promise "to tell the truth, the whole truth, and nothing but the truth." But what does it mean to speak "the whole truth"?

There is a big difference between the whole truth and everyday facts. We all could list a hundred facts about ourselves, such as our age, hair color, and weight. But what is the whole truth about who we are? Surely we are more than a collection of measurable data. For example, we have mixed motives, many emotions, and doubt as well as faith. None of us fully knows even ourselves. Nearly everything—from historical events to God—exists as only part of the complex "whole truth" that is beyond humans' limited understanding.

Nevertheless, we sometimes make big-picture claims about aspects of the whole truth. We Christians offer such claims based not on our own knowledge but on God's revealed (or spoken) truth.

God-talk addresses this big picture, including who God is, who we humans are, what has gone wrong with God's good creation, and why a faithful God sacrificed his Son. As explained earlier, our understandings of such great topics constitute our control beliefs. More than just facts, they are deep truths that equip us to penetrate the surface of mere human understanding. Whenever we express such God-revealed truth verbally or nonverbally, we use God-talk.

Speakers can be factual, honest, and earnest without addressing their big-picture assumptions. They might not even be aware that they have control beliefs, as if their facts alone speak for themselves. For example, whenever we hear a speaker use words such as *natural, normal,* and *solution,* we ought to beware. What is truly natural or normal for humans? What is human nature? Will the speaker's solutions for human problems create new problems?

As servant speakers, we first should listen and dialogue with others to clarify what they ultimately believe. We then need to begin determining why, when, and how to use God-talk, which is believers' foundation for big-picture truth. As we speak with others and listen to their responses, some of our views might change. We might especially refine our control beliefs, thereby making us wiser speakers in the future.

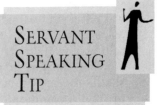

SERVANT SPEAKING TIP

Avoid inappropriate or confusing God-talk when addressing nonreligious groups on nonreligious topics.

Of course, explicit God-talk can offend as well as serve particular audiences. Knowing our control beliefs does not give us license to rattle them off arrogantly whenever we desire. Loose God-talk can confuse as well as insult coworkers, friends, and even honest inquirers about the faith.

When I used the term *sin* in a presentation to a professional communication association, an attendee challenged my "religious bias." A few heads nodded in agreement. Although I see sin as the root problem in human communication, I realized that this word probably had elicited many interpretations based on audience members' upbringings and stereotypes.

Rather than quickly trying to explain the gospel and define sin, I admitted, "You're right. This *is* one of my biases. So how about if we just agree that human communication is broken, even if we differ on the cause. Okay?" He agreed, and the group quickly moved on to other questions and discussion. I should have been more audience-sensitive in my speech, but at least I had left the door open for attendees to later converse with me about my "bias."

During an intense discussion between angry parents and a defensive principal at a Christian school meeting, a speaker reminded everyone that school administrators and parents alike are fallen creatures who do not always act in tune with their faith. He rightly sought to overcome the parent versus administrator mentality that was pitting the two sides against each other as if only one side were correct. In this case, God-talk was fitting. But in a less religious setting, it would not have been appropriate let alone effective.

When speaking to non-Christian audiences, believers usually should replace explicitly religious words with those that might provide a common ground for discussion. The point is not to dilute truth but to offer listeners a meaningful bridge from their everyday lives to biblical reality. Otherwise audiences might be turned off by our seemingly tribal or self-righteous language.

Everyday God-talk requires us to learn how to identify new metaphors for age-old control beliefs. We should ask ourselves, What is the root meaning of a biblical word or phrase? How can we capture some of that word's meaning for a particular nonreligious audience? Here are some examples of religious terms translated for nonreligious groups:

- Jesus Christ = God
- sin = brokenness
- religion = spirituality
- obedience = responsibility
- salvation = peace and justice
- sacrifice = selfless love
- church = faith community
- guilt = conscience

When we speak to civic or business groups, then, we should normally refrain from explicit God-talk unless we are asked to give a more personal or faith-related presentation. Even then, we need to use God-talk carefully, defining key terms and admitting, when appropriate, that Christians also sometimes disagree on important matters.

Doubt-Talk—Speaking within the Limits of Human Knowing

One of the most historically provable control beliefs is that humans are not all-knowing. Compared with God, we are significantly ignorant, regardless of our formal education or everyday knowledge. Our public speech especially needs to account for these limitations.

Doubting some of our own rhetoric helps us to be honest and accountable. We might speak positively about the role of religion in society, for example, but we should admit that even the most religious people and institutions can act foolishly. Knowing and believing our basic control beliefs is one thing; applying them perfectly in specific speeches is far more complicated.

Christ addressed Pharisees and Sadducees who dogmatically claimed to know every nuance of God's Word and will. Pharisees did not live up to their own legalistic rhetoric. Sadducees taught false doctrine. Unwilling to practice doubt-talk, both groups self-righteously equated their own flawed pronouncements with ultimate truth.

SERVANT SPEAKING TIP

"I don't know for sure" is the truest thing to say when you are uncertain.

Today, the lack of doubt-talk is starkly evident in many disputes within churches and across denominations. Some people even use public prayers to advance their own agendas. Preachers on occasion interpret Scripture in tune with their pet projects and political or social biases. I have heard ministers proclaim that America is the one Christian nation, when in fact Christianity is spreading like wildfire in parts of Latin America, Africa, and Asia.

We should not be afraid to take a stand. Whenever we go beyond our control beliefs, however, we should check our sources. When in doubt, we should consider adding a phrase such as "it appears to me" or "I could be mistaken." We just might be.

Honest-Talk—Avoiding Intentional Deception

Speaking truthfully includes honesty. It is one thing to be uncertain and something quite worse to deceive someone knowingly. A lie is a statement intended to deceive, regardless of whether the statement is ultimately true. Honest-talk avoids intentional deception.

Questions to Ask to Avoid Deceptive Use of Sources

- Have I used all sources fairly without twisting their words or including only the material that supports my thesis?

- Have I researched and examined sources that hold views contrary to those of my selected sources and my thesis?

- Have I represented my sources' credentials fairly?

Because much early rhetoric was meant to help legal courts discern truth amid competing claims, lying was unacceptable. As ancient rhetoric moved beyond the courts, however, some public orators focused more on power, success, and personal fame than on honesty. In Plato's *Republic*, Socrates criticizes those who captured the souls of young men with false statements and boastful speeches.[5]

These ancient deceivers, generally associated with the Second Sophistic (50–250), tarnished the public reputation of rhetoricians for centuries. They gave the word *eloquence* a bad name by reducing it to "effective" speech regardless of truthfulness. Yet today the words *sophist* and *rhetoric* both connote intentional deception.[6]

Paul distanced himself from "mere eloquence" to show that he cared about honesty as well as impact. He reminded the Corinthians that he had preached the gospel to them "free of charge," indicating that selling rhetorical techniques was then an issue among religious speakers (2 Cor. 11:7).

Two centuries later, Augustine grew increasingly uneasy with orators who advocated any message for a fee. Calling them "word vendors," Augustine said that their reputation "was high in proportion to" their "success in deceiving people." Disheartened by the lack of honesty in his profession, he decided to retire quietly from his post as a "salesman of words in the markets of rhetoric."[7]

In both the Old and the New Testament, honesty is praised and dishonesty is condemned. "Whoever would love life and see good days must keep . . . his lips from deceitful speech" (1 Pet. 3:10). A good person speaks "truth from his heart" (Ps. 15:2).

One of the Ten Commandments even highlights the sin of false testimony. It refers partly to what Zechariah called giving "true and sound judgment" in court (8:16). Today's laws against slander (speaking falsely about someone to a third party) and libel (writing falsely about someone) reflect the influence of biblical morality. The purpose of this commandment was not just to discourage deception but also to encourage truth telling. The Heidelberg Catechism said in the sixteenth century that Christians should avoid lying and deception of all kinds because they are tools of the devil, the great deceiver. But it added that Christians should "love the truth, speak it uprightly and confess it."

Plagiarism

Plagiarism is passing off someone else's ideas and expressions as one's own. Failing to give credit to the source of an idea is a common form of plagiarism. So is using specific material from someone else's publications or speeches without acknowledging that person as the source.

Fabrication

Fabrication is making up data, examples, findings, or other information. Unintentional fabrication includes uncritically accepting as fact what someone else says through primary or secondary research. Virtually every speech topic includes widely cited urban legends that people mistake as facts (e.g., Eskimos have dozens of words for snow, a company's logo is a satanic symbol, a microwave oven cooks food from the

SERVANT SPEAKING TIP

Mention the sources of ideas, quotations, and definitions used in your speeches, including each major source's credentials.

inside out, and backward masking of musical recordings communicates subliminally to listeners).

One way to avoid even unintentional fabrication is by checking secondary sources against primary ones. If one source quotes another source, verify the original. When this is not possible, honest-talk requires a speaker to acknowledge that the quotation is taken from a secondary source.

The Internet, in particular, easily spreads data and quotations without the scrutiny of a careful editor. Fortunately, websites exist that are dedicated to determining the truthfulness of widely quoted but rarely sourced statements supposedly made by historical persons. For example, there are sites where scholars evaluate the veracity of quotations supposedly made by Augustine and St. Francis of Assisi. According to one of the sites, a popular quotation attributed to St. Francis probably is not his: "Preach the gospel always; if necessary, use words." We know that St. Francis said similar things, but the experts have not been able to verify this well-liked quotation appearing on posters and greeting cards as well as widely cited in sermons and books.

Another important way to avoid fabrication is by checking a source's credentials before referring to that source in a speech or handout. One popular Christian speaker and radio personality refers to himself as "Dr." even though he has only a law degree. Since lawyers rarely refer to themselves as doctors of jurisprudence, this person might be using the title deceptively to enhance his credibility when speaking and writing about subjects that have little to do with the law.

Justifiable Deception

Christians have long debated when intentional deception might be justified. A few biblical passages seem to suggest that lying might rarely be acceptable. For instance, Rahab evidently pleased God when she misdirected spies (James 2:25). But her deception was not public; it was intended only for a small group and a special, God-sanctioned purpose. The New Testament offers no clear justifications for deception, but we do justify it in situations when telling the truth might lead to catastrophic results, such as the death of innocent people. The lesson seems to be that lying ought to be rare and focused. Even then, there is no justification for evil motives.

Some speakers seem to justify white lies—fibs of little moral importance that everyone more or less accepts for their illustrative value. For instance, speakers embellish real or fictional stories to make them more engaging and to clarify the point of a story. Many fine speakers also use hyperbolic language such as "always," "tremendous," and "forever" for emphasis.

For example, a host might exaggerate slightly when introducing a speaker. A host also might publicly thank a speaker who failed to serve the audience well. Overlooking someone's foibles is usually kindness rather than evil deception.

> ### SERVANT SPEAKING TIP
>
> Learn to locate the fine line between acceptable exaggeration and unacceptable deception by sharing your ethical dilemmas in advance with trusted friends. Would they feel deceived?

Excessively kind words, however, can blossom into misleading flattery. The psalmist says that "flattering lips speak with deception" (12:2).

Servant speakers praise others appropriately, not excessively. When a friend agreed to deliver the eulogy at the funeral of her 102-year-old grandfather, she fittingly focused on his virtues rather than his weaknesses. The noble purpose of the eulogy was to give thanks to God for a man who, in spite of his brokenness, had blessed so many and remained so faithful. It would have been inappropriate to be critical of him at such a celebration.

Speakers who venture beyond acceptable white lies risk tarnishing their *ethos*. Honest-talk builds trust between speaker and audience, whereas dishonesty eventually discredits speakers while disserving their misinformed audiences.

Straight-Talk—Using Clear, Plain Language

A well-known communication scholar presented his latest research about the effects of television viewing on children. The

WAYS OF FOSTERING STRAIGHT-TALK

- stating and restating your thesis during a speech
- defining important terms
- employing relevant examples and illustrations
- matching the complexity of your language to the audience

lecture was filled with technical jargon and qualifying terms such as *usually, sometimes,* and *apparently.*

After he wrapped up the lecture, there was an uncomfortably long period of silence before one professor finally spoke up: "Sir, I have always appreciated your work. I especially liked your clear notion about how the media affect children. But now I think you've lost your notion!" The seminar room erupted in laughter, and the speaker good-heartedly joined in: "You know, I thought I had a notion when I woke up this morning to prepare for the lecture. But I guess I lost it!" His humble response elicited a fruitful discussion that clarified his thesis.

Audiences rightly expect clear, plain speech. Aristotle held that one of the three virtues of style is clarity. Excessively flowery words and arcane ideas sometimes temporarily impress listeners, but they never really serve them.

Moreover, some presenters intentionally seem to say little. They circle around the main point without addressing it directly. Politicians, for example, sometimes seem to be adept at speaking a lot without saying much.

The imprecise use of important terms is particularly confusing. Careless speakers toss around words such as *freedom, equality,* and *individual rights* without explaining them clearly. Preachers might fail to define biblical and theological terms.

Of course, audiences are obliged to pay attention and to strive to understand a speaker. Yet speakers need to be aware of their audience's ability to grasp complicated material. Therefore, speakers should observe audience members for any signs of confusion or frustration. When audience members are having trouble understanding, they start daydreaming, looking at their watches, and whispering among themselves. Occasionally, they leave! Straight-talk, by contrast, generally draws in an audience.

Some communication experts say that a human being "cannot not communicate." They rightly argue that any verbal or nonverbal cue—such as a quivering voice or a frown—can influence an audience's perceptions of a speaker. An audience, however, might not interpret such cues as the speaker intends. If a speaker frowns, for example, he or she might be expressing negative feelings or simply having trouble reading the speech because of insufficient lighting. Since communication is shared understanding, not merely one-way effect, we can inadvertently miscommunicate (or unintentionally lead an audience to interpret us incorrectly).

Servant speakers aim for straight-talk to be true to others. They avoid verbal and nonverbal messages that even unintentionally mislead listeners. They mean what they say and say what they mean to the best of their abilities. Biblically speaking, their yes means yes, and their no means no (Matt. 5:37; James 5:12).

Conclusion

Servant speakers are truth tellers. As good listeners, they seek to be well-informed so as not to mislead their audience-neighbors. They avoid deception except in rare cases, such as when lives might be at stake. Although puffed-up flattery is common, servant speakers try to be kind without slipping into boastful language. They also seek to be as lucid as possible, helping listeners to understand them.

Committed to their big-picture control beliefs, servant speakers nevertheless doubt some of their own rhetoric. They know that they, too, are fallen creatures who cannot grasp the whole truth apart from what is revealed in God's Word. Therefore, they acknowledge their own ignorance even while humbly seeking to be true to God, their audience, and themselves.

Was the commencement speaker's high school run like a prison? Was the comparison appropriate for the event? The student speaker had an obligation to be honest and straight with his audience but also to doubt some of his own rhetoric for the sake of serving the assembly gathered for a graduation celebration.

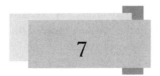

7

BEING VIRTUOUS

A friend attended a lecture by a prominent biblical creationist. After being introduced, the speaker rapidly delivered a well-rehearsed slide show that did not address some of the major disparities between scientific findings and a literal reading of the Bible. So when the speaker finished and the host opened the floor for questions, my friend spoke up. The dialogue went something like this:

"Thank you for your overview, but could you address the current disagreements between many scientists and creationists? For example, what about using various scientific techniques to determine the age of the earth?"

"Those are irrelevant findings," replied the presenter. "After all, who speaks the truth, almighty God or secular scientists? The Bible is our textbook. Next question."

So began a Q&A that pleased some attendees and frustrated others. My friend later told me that this event turned her off to the speaker. Whether the creationist's arguments were right or wrong, she worried that his dismissive attitude toward critics would discredit Christianity.

Servant speakers seek to be both *effective* communicators and *virtuous* persons. Their verbal and nonverbal language demonstrates the fruit of the Spirit in their lives.

Ethos versus Persona

Today, Hollywood celebrities, corporate executives, and national politicians often hire publicists to manage their persona—a fabricated and managed public image. The idea is to project a positive image regardless of what the person is really like.

For a servant speaker, however, inner character, not external persona, is foundational. In fact, throughout history, many rhetoricians believed that a speaker's *ethos* (how an audience perceives a speaker's personal character) should reflect the inner heart. Orators were obligated to be worthy of an audience's confidence and trust, convincing listeners partly by being intrinsically good persons, not just by projecting a credible public image.

The ancient Greeks and Romans as well as later Christian philosophers spoke of virtues—good qualities of character. For instance, being a justice-loving and honest person was thought to be more virtuous than being an unfair and deceitful one. Virtues were seen as character traits that spring from a speaker's heart and shape his or her actions. Good people tend to act rightly.

Servant speakers gain integrity by unifying their inner and outer selves, by *being* virtuous as well as by *acting* virtuously. Teachers, for example, "speak" with their attitudes, not just their words. When their character contradicts what they teach, they lose credibility; such "dis-integrated" teachers no longer embody virtue.

Paul describes Christian virtues as fruit of the Spirit: love, joy, peace, patience, kindness, goodness, faithfulness, gentleness, and self-control (Gal. 5:22). These qualities should form the inner character and shape the outer actions of servant speakers. "May the words of my mouth and the meditation of my heart be pleasing in your sight," says the psalmist (19:14). Mouth and heart are meant to work together in communication. Since this book addresses self-sacrificial love throughout, the present chapter focuses on other speech-relevant fruit of the Spirit.

Joy

Servant speakers joyfully serve an audience because they know that their knowledge, skills, and audience are all gifts. Even though we should work hard to hone our speech, the capacity for serving audiences is a God-given gift. Joy-shaped speech flows naturally from a heart of gratitude.

We all prefer speakers who enjoy addressing us. Speakers cannot completely concoct a joyful spirit, although sometimes they have to go through the motions because their own lives are disheartening. Whenever we sense that a speaker is not taking pleasure in the task, we wonder, Does the speaker care? Is the speaker grateful for the opportunity? Does he or she value our attention?

Students naturally like teachers who enjoy teaching, just as congregants appreciate preachers whose joyful spirits shape their style of delivery. A person's joyful countenance elicits pleasure in audiences as long as it seems honest and it is fitting to the situation.

One way of bringing more joy into the art of researching and delivering speeches is to focus on subjects that we truly take pleasure in learning and talking about. Another way is helping others do so, such as in group presentations or by tutoring and mentoring students. In fact, teaching is one of the best ways of learning. A third way to enhance our joy is to select topics and theses that we know will serve audiences; one of the rewards for servant speaking is the delight received from loving our audience-neighbors as ourselves.

Servant speakers do not create the gift of speech. Nor do they teach themselves everything they know about speaking well. Recognizing that servant speaking is a gift, they joyfully serve their audiences as neighbors.

Peace

Servant speakers promote relational harmony, which the Old Testament calls shalom.[1] They see their speaking abilities partly as means for reconciliation. They are not adverse to confrontation, but they realize that when and how they communicate are

Shalom Is Relational Harmony . . .

- among people
- between people and God
- between people and the physical creation
- between individuals and their own selves

critically important factors for fostering true peace in which people can flourish, not merely pretend to get along.

When Cicero spoke of the goal of pleasing an audience, he meant more than fun or entertainment. His Latin concept of pleasure meant "delight" or "enjoyment." In other words, speakers should connect pleasingly with audiences rather than frustrate or irritate them; speakers should be conciliatory.[2]

Scripture calls speakers to promote peace by avoiding intentionally divisive language. A servant speaker internally adopts, externally lives, and mildly speaks the peace of Christ, even when the consequences could be personally grave. Stephen, the first Christian martyr, was stoned for his peaceful testimony on behalf of his murderers.

Yet some people approach public discourse with a warlike attitude designed to belittle and even destroy "enemies." They seem bent on promoting conflict. Many radio and TV talk shows have become verbal slugfests with individuals interrupting one another to land spoken punches.

Sometimes even soft-spoken and seemingly sincere speakers intend to spread disharmony. The psalmist says that a person's speech can be "smooth as butter" even though he has "war" in his heart and his words are "drawn swords" (55:21). This kind of militant rhetoric is not playful banter, humorous wordplay, or respectful disagreement. Rather, it is meant to hurt opponents. Combative speech might help a speaker win a few verbal skirmishes, but in the long run, it leads to distrust and disharmony. That is not the way language is supposed to be used by peaceful people, even when they disagree and debate.

Patience

Servant speakers are patient, attending to God's timing (*kairos*) rather than just their own. Those of us in industrialized nations frequently find that day-to-day demands leave little time for culti-

STEPHEN RESPONDS TO HIS MURDERERS

When they heard this, they were furious and gnashed their teeth at him. But Stephen, full of the Holy Spirit, looked up to heaven and saw the glory of God, and Jesus standing at the right hand of God. "Look," he said, "I see heaven open and the Son of Man standing at the right hand of God."

At this they covered their ears and, yelling at the top of their voices, they all rushed at him, dragged him out of the city and began to stone him. . . .

While they were stoning him, Stephen prayed, "Lord Jesus, receive my spirit." Then he fell on his knees and cried out, "Lord, do not hold this sin against them." When he had said this, he fell asleep.

Acts 7:54–60

vating patience. Aleksandr Solzhenitsyn told Harvard University graduates that hastiness is a "psychic disease" of our era.[3]

Public speakers, too, often become impatient. Some employ charged language to conquer audiences quickly. High-profile, big-fee speakers occasionally zip in and out of scheduled presentations without offering time to dialogue. They rev up audiences and dismiss listeners who are struggling to articulate questions or concerns. They don't have time to listen!

Of course, excessive busyness and the resulting impatience are nothing new. Søren Kierkegaard writes that "in the world of spirit, busyness, keeping up with others, hustling hither and yon, makes it almost impossible for an individual to form a heart, to

> ## SERVANT SPEAKING TIP
>
> To foster patience during Q&A after a speech, assume that any miscommunication during the speech was your own fault rather than the fault of the audience.

become a responsible, alive self." He adds, "It is absolutely unethical when one is so busy communicating that he forgets to be what he teaches."[4]

In the New Testament, the word *servant* partly means "waiting on" others. This language survives in English with reference to restaurant servers who wait on customers. Servant speakers avoid cutting corners by setting aside time for researching, crafting, and rehearsing each presentation. They also deliver speeches patiently enough so that an audience has time to follow along, gain understanding, and formulate responses. Finally, they wait on God's timing.

God-sensitive patience seems a bit far-fetched in today's time-crazed culture. However, it actually enables speakers to remain attentive to Spirit-led opportunities. When servant speakers trust God, the Spirit speaks through them (Matt. 10:20).

During a heated civic meeting, a citizen remained calm while the audience became increasingly impatient. As the discussion waned with no sign of a resolution, he quietly rose and suggested that we try to do what was right for the city overall rather than for any of the competing factions. To my astonishment, everyone agreed, the major issue was resolved, participants shook hands, and the meeting was adjourned. Later, I realized that it was less the force of the rhetoric than the timing that made the difference. People were tired of haggling and still hoped to work out a compromise, but no one seemed willing to seize the opportunity. Perhaps the citizen had been led by the Spirit.

The opposite of patient speech is hasty, often hot-tempered and ill-considered rhetoric. This might include inappropriate jokes, humorous put-downs, and snappy retorts, especially during impromptu speeches and Q&A sessions. Proverbs says that there is "more hope for a fool" than for someone who speaks hastily (29:20).

Kindness

A servant's speech conveys sincere kindness toward others. Kindness is honoring others in verbal and nonverbal actions. Public kindness is often called civility.

People sometimes have difficulty conversing civilly. Christians, too, occasionally justify unkind language. We find ourselves ridiculing others with a nasty quip or a demeaning expression.

A trial attorney told me that he really dislikes making the opposing side look like fools, even though that is his job. "I'm not sure that's your occupation," I replied. "If people acted foolishly, you should point that out for the sake of justice." The real issue, it seemed to me, is how to expose others' foolishness without calling them fools, to honor *them* but not their improper *actions*.

Kind speech does not always come easy, especially when we feel we are on a mission to persuade others. A non-Christian friend complained about a wedding he attended where the pastor pleaded for attendees to accept Jesus or risk going to hell in the near future. Did he display kindness by preaching hell and damnation at a celebrative event? Could he have presented the love of Christ in a much kinder fashion? Was the gospel inappropriate at such an event?

> ## SERVANT SPEAKING TIP
>
> Be sensitive to *kairos,* a special moment when the Spirit might pave the way for you to speak what is needed.

COMMON TYPES OF UNKIND SPEECH

- ridiculing: making fun of others

- mocking: negatively caricaturing someone's peculiarities

- gossiping: talking about people behind their backs

The creationist speaker mentioned earlier apparently knew his material well, but he lacked kindness toward those in his audience who did not already agree with his conclusions about when God made the world. He dismissed those who were honestly grappling with the subject.

Augustine posted the following sentence in large letters on the wall in his room: "Here we do not speak evil of anyone." In tune with such a good reminder, I programmed my cell phone to display the following message every time I look at the screen to place a call: SHALOM.

Goodness

Servant speakers use audience-sensitive words and examples. Since audience members are their neighbors, they avoid offending them with morally inappropriate speech.

I grew up in a working-class family that frequently used obscenity and profanity. Off-color jokes were especially common among men. I realize today how dramatically my standards of good speech have changed when I happen upon one of the comedy TV channels, where some jokes include cuss words, sexual innuendos, bathroom humor, and outrageous profanity.

Before I cleaned up my language, however, I offended audiences with what I incorrectly assumed were innocuous references. I tried to justify such language by pointing out that Scripture and various well-known writers, including Shakespeare, sometimes used similar references.

COMMON TYPES OF BAD SPEECH

- obscenity: immodest, indecent talk
- profanity: language that disrespects God and religion
- perversity: corrupt, wicked speech

There are nearly always more positive and less offensive ways of expressing the same thing. Servant speakers do not need to be prudish or Pollyannaish, but neither should they rub listeners the wrong way with inappropriate words and examples. They should be too good-hearted to want to do anything inappropriate.

Gentleness

Gentleness is vital for servant speakers. Paul appealed to the Corinthians "by the meekness and gentleness of Christ" (2 Cor. 10:1). "A gentle tongue can break a bone," says Proverbs (25:15). Gentle speakers are mild-mannered toward audience-neighbors, even as they sometimes make forcefully persuasive arguments.

During the Victorian era, gentleness was associated with upper-class, refined persons, with gentlemen and gentlewomen preoccupied with socially proper mores. Jesus instead associated gentleness with humble speech that "touches" rather than pushes others.

While strolling down Bourbon Street in New Orleans one evening, I came across three young street preachers. People laughed in their faces and tossed beer at them. Some women irreverently pulled up their blouses.

Eventually, the evangelists found someone who was willing to listen—or so they thought. Sitting on the curb was a very inebriated, college-age guy desperately trying to stand up on his own. He was not making much headway when the evangelists descended upon him and began yelling at him. As one evangelist ratcheted up his sermon, the intoxicated man mumbled incoherently and tried to wave away the preacher with his unstable arms. Then the other two evangelists grabbed the reveler by the shoulders to hold him still so they could jam a Bible tract down his shirt. I wondered why they did not instead help the man with gentle words and kind deeds.

The episode reminded me that a mild-mannered spirit is better than an overbearing one. As Augustine told Christian speakers, a gentle person does not revel in controversy.[5] Gentleness is one kind of loving witness. Peter says that we should be prepared to give an answer to those who ask the reason for our hope; he adds that we should respond gently (1 Pet. 3:15). Paul encourages believers to make their gentleness evident to all (Phil. 4:5).

Faithfulness

Every speech is an act of faith, since we cannot guarantee our intended results. We all know from experience that communication is sloppy and somewhat unpredictable. Yet we carry on. No matter how hard they work, faithful speakers trust the Spirit to guide their work. In fact, they work hard to speak well because they are called to persevere faithfully with God.

Eugene Peterson realized as a young preacher that members of his congregation were yawning and sleeping. One woman gave him hope; every Sunday she took extensive sermon notes in shorthand. Peterson eventually learned that "she was getting ready to leave her husband and was using the hour of worship to practice her shorthand so she could get a self-supporting job."[6]

Once I drove several hours to speak at a large church. As I pulled into the parking lot, I was delighted to see that nearly every spot was filled. I parked, found the door to the fellowship hall, and discovered three people sitting at a table. One of them smiled and warmly welcomed me. Then she apologized for the poor attendance and quickly offered a litany of all the ways the publicity team had promoted the event.

"But it looks like a great crowd," I replied. "Well," she said sheepishly, "all the cars you saw outside belong to the people attending the Alcoholics Anonymous meeting upstairs. We three event planners are the only ones here for your presentation."

If we believe primarily in ourselves or our audiences, we are bound to be disappointed. We need more than skill, self-confidence, and audience applause. We need faith in a God who can speak through us and guarantee truly worthwhile results.

Faithfulness also includes being true to our audiences. When we promise to speak at a given time and place, we need to be there. When we accept an invitation to address a group or are required by our job or school to make a presentation, we should to do so to the best of our abilities. Shoddy speeches are not just a waste of an audience's time; they fail to serve that audience.

Finally, we should be faithful to ourselves, both by believing in our God-
given abilities to serve others and by
following through on the promises we
make to ourselves to serve them. When
we commit ourselves to plan or practice
a speech, for example, we should do so
wholeheartedly.

SERVANT SPEAKING TIP

Even when speaking off-the-cuff, listen to yourself before uttering words. Be your own best censor.

Self-Control

Our tongues are restless. They seem
to have a will of their own, causing us
to say things we later regret.

Every speech is an opportunity to regulate our communication. Servant speakers practice self-control—self-censorship of
what they say and how they say it on behalf of an audience.
Without self-control, speakers are more prone to get into re-
grettable trouble. For instance, we might say too much, violate
others' privacy, belittle people, and twist the truth, sometimes
with admirable motives.

Simply put, we should think before speaking in order to con-
form our words to our faith. "If anyone considers himself religious and yet does not keep a tight rein on his tongue, he deceives
himself and his religion is worthless," warns James (1:26).

Impromptu and extemporaneous speaking are most likely to
cause us to wish we had greater self-control. It is so easy to put
our foot in our mouth. This is partly why speech preparation is
essential. Even five minutes of thought and an outline quickly
jotted on a napkin before an impromptu speech at a wedding,
birthday celebration, or family reunion are helpful. We need to
rehearse extemporaneous speeches, even though we will never
deliver the same speech twice in exactly the same manner. Lastly,
self-control calls us to listen to ourselves as we speak, editing
ourselves as we hear the words developing in our minds before
uttering them.

An ancient Jewish teaching says that the human tongue is like
an arrow, not just a sword (Pss. 57:4; 64:3). A rabbi explains that
"if a man unsheathes his sword to kill his friend, and his friend

pleads with him and begs for mercy, the man may be mollified and return the sword to its scabbard." Once an arrow is shot, however, "it cannot be returned, no matter how much one wants to."[7] Without self-control, we become verbal archers who sometimes wish we could put our arrows back into our quivers.

Conclusion

The Christian faith offers a wealth of wisdom about being a virtuous speaker. It reminds us that servant speaking is a matter of character as well as of skill. We cannot be perfect persons, but we can learn to be more virtuous speakers by studying and imitating saintly ones.

Jesus is our greatest model for virtue, but he had many advantages over us, including knowing his audiences perfectly. Jesus lived in complete intimacy with the Father and the Spirit; he had immediate access to each human being's personality and yearnings. Therefore, we should also look to imperfect but faithful servant speakers such as Moses, Paul, Augustine, and others we should admire.

As Paul puts it, servant speakers are part of the message. Their inner character speaks intentionally and unintentionally. They become what Paul calls God's "letters," with their "text" written in their hearts and communicated through their character as well as their actions (2 Cor. 3:1–3). The speaker who addressed creationism apparently forgot that the quality of his character was just as important as the content of his formal message. He failed to serve his audience and to honor God most fully.

Appendix A

Checklist for Preparing a Speech

___ I determined the *audience's* topical knowledge, feelings, and expectations for the occasion (see appendix C).

___ I established a clear *purpose* for serving my audience-neighbors (e.g., to inform, persuade, or delight).

___ I stated my *thesis* in one clear, specific sentence.

___ I consulted credible primary and secondary *sources* on the topic (see appendix B).

___ I used credible sources *ethically* as representative of the views presented in the research (without fabrication or plagiarism).

___ I wrote and revised a sentence *outline* for each main point.

___ I practiced delivering a speech *introduction* that will gain audience interest, establish my servant ethos, present my purpose and thesis, offer a preview, and transition to the body of the speech.

___ I *organized* the speech logically (e.g., simple, dialectical, or problem-solution logic), with clear transitions between main points, adequate reviews of previous points, and a memorable visual metaphor, keyword acronym, or sequential numbering for main points.

___ I found illustrative *stories* that relate to my main points and will interest my audience; I practiced telling them extemporaneously to friends or coworkers

___ I prepared appropriate *technology,* including slideware (PowerPoint, audio, video) and other media, such as paper handouts, black and white boards, artifacts, and foam boards (see appendix D).

___ I determined how to *speak truthfully* with appropriate God-talk (including control beliefs), doubt-talk, honest-talk, and straight-talk.

___ I *practiced* the speech with friends or classmates to become more verbally and nonverbally expressive (without hesitation and verbal fillers) and to hear positive and negative feedback for revision.

___ I anticipated three major *audience questions* and prepared answers.

Appendix B

Checklist for Topic Research

____ I narrowed my speech topic so I could research it well without being swamped with unmanageable quantities of information.

____ I refined the topic as I reviewed primary and secondary sources.

____ I made sure that the refined topic is relevant to representatives of the likely audience (i.e., I discussed the topic with people who represent the audience, or I found secondary sources that discuss the relevance of the topic for this kind of audience).

____ I searched relevant secondary sources (e.g., scholarly books, professional journals, trade books, popular magazines, newspapers, reference works, and the Internet).

____ In the case of information found on the Internet (not private databases available only at or through libraries), I verified the sources and evaluated the sources' credibility.

____ I interviewed via telephone, email, postal mail, or in person authorities on the topic and secured their permission before quoting them.

____ Where relevant, I sought information and perspective from Christian as well as mainstream authorities on the topic.

____ I found and considered information contrary to my thesis.

____ I made copies of secondary sources and took careful notes of primary research so as to be able to defend my use of these sources.

___ I determined how to refer to sources in the speech without giving full bibliographic references for all information (i.e., I can explain my primary and secondary sources while not detracting from the flow of my speech).

___ I gained enough knowledge of the topic that I know what I am talking about and what I should not talk about.

Appendix C

Checklist for Audience Research

___ I described the profile of my audience-neighbors in one sentence with enough specificity that I can imagine who they are (e.g., their demographics, interests, values, and concerns).

___ I determined why this audience would want to listen to me, what it would assume about me, and what it might expect from me.

___ I spoke with people who represent the audience (according to the above profile), asking them for their feelings about the topic, how I might serve them, and what they would say if they were to give such a speech.

___ I searched secondary sources for information about what the audience likely knows or assumes regarding the topic. If the information seemed contradictory or incomplete, I shared it with likely representatives of the audience to gain their insights.

___ If possible, I spoke in advance with someone who will be in the actual audience.

___ If possible, I spoke with the person who invited me to give the speech to clarify his or her expectations.

___ If possible, I shared an outline or draft of the speech in advance with representatives of the audience to get their feelings about how I could better serve them.

____ I reviewed the language and visual illustrations in the speech
to make sure that none of the material will offend the
audience, seeking advice as needed from representatives of the
audience.

____ If appropriate, I considered the feelings of the audience
toward issues of faith, especially the use of God-talk.

____ As I became more audience focused, I imagined myself as a
member of this group and sought to serve my audience-
neighbors as I would want to be served.

Appendix D

Using Slideware Wisely

Aesthetics. Design slides that are simple (no "noisy" backgrounds or excessive graphics), pleasing to the eye (not stuffy, just clean and attractive), and readable. Avoid high-tech bells and whistles that might impress audiences but detract from communication.

Continuity. Practice running the slides seamlessly as you practice your speech to overcome visual or verbal hesitations. If possible, use a wireless mouse/remote control. If not, practice with a friend who can advance the slides from the back of the room according to your unobtrusive visual cues (such as eye contact). Do not repeat phrases such as "next," "here we see," and "this is" when you transition from slide to slide.

Effectiveness. Rather than turning immediately to digital media, consider whether other media would be more effective, such as black and white boards, poster boards, simple artifacts, and paper handouts (the latter are especially good for simple outlines, lists of sources, definitions of key words/concepts, and lengthy source quotations).

Focus. Direct the audience's attention to a slide by pointing to it with your entire arm. If possible, use a laser pointer to spot the relevant part of the slide. When you are not using a slide during the speech, either mute the projector or plan ahead by including black slides as transitions. As a last resort, leave the slide on the screen lit, but when you are not using it, walk away from the screen to draw attention to yourself. When there are many things for the audience to look at on a slide, you should focus members' attention verbally and nonverbally on the proper section.

Legality. Never use copyrighted images or text without the permission of the owner. Most images on the Web, for instance, are not in public domain.

Preparation. Test the slides on the computer and projector that are available at the speech venue. Be ready to present in case the technology breaks down. Paper handouts of important slides are usually an adequate backup.

Relevance. Integrate slides (and video/audio clips) sparingly into your speech only at relevant points, especially for examples or illustrations. Less is more. Never merely read what is on slides as if the slides are your speech text.

Significance. Use a slide only when it contributes significantly to the relevant point; avoid trite use even if the slide is relevant.

Appendix E

Form for Evaluating Speeches

Date: **Length** (in minutes):

Title:

Speaker's Name and Position:

Occasion (Where and when was the speech?)

Purpose (How did the speaker intend to serve audience-neighbors?)

Thesis (What was the speaker's one-sentence thesis?)

Introduction (Did the speaker quickly gain audience interest, establish a servant *ethos*, state a purpose, present a thesis, offer a preview, and transition to the body of the speech?)

Conclusion (Did the speaker restate the thesis, summarize main points, and, if suitable, call the audience to know, believe, or act?)

Sources (Did the speech and Q&A demonstrate that the speaker had listened adequately to primary and secondary sources?)

Technology (Did the speaker use media/technologies appropriately, smoothly, and attractively?)

Organization (Did the speaker use simple, dialectical, or problem-solution logic along with transitions, summaries, and memorable keyword acronyms, visual metaphors, or sequential numbering?)

Verbal Expressiveness (Was the speaker's vocal delivery aptly energetic, impassioned, and engaging without hesitancy, monotone, and verbal fillers?)

Nonverbal Expressiveness (Did the speaker maintain eye contact and use arms and body effectively in support of verbal expressiveness?)

Virtue (Did the speaker's ethos reflect relevant fruit of the Spirit: love, joy, peace, patience, kindness, goodness, gentleness, faithfulness, and self-control?)

Truth Telling (Did the speaker appropriately use God-talk, honest-talk, doubt-talk, and straight-talk?)

Storytelling (Did the speaker creatively tell fitting stories?)

The following served the audience well:

The following required additional attention:

Appendix F

Sample Speech Outline Elements

I. Introduction
   A. Expression of gratitude or other acknowledgment of audience and occasion
   B. Story, anecdote, or interesting information to engage audience-neighbors
   C. Statement of purpose
   D. Statement of thesis
   E. Preview of speech
   F. Transition to body of speech and the first main point
II. Body
   A. First subpoint
      1. Examples, illustrations, stories, facts, etc., in support of point
      2. Summary of first subpoint
      3. Transition to next subpoint
   B. Repeat A above for each subpoint, expanding summaries to include all the previous subpoints, and final transition to conclusion
III. Conclusion
   A. Review or summary of main points
   B. Restatement of thesis
   C. Call for audience response
   D. Restatement of gratitude to audience and reference to occasion as appropriate

NOTES

Chapter 1

1. Aleksandr Solzhenitsyn, *A World Split Apart* (New York: Harper & Row, 1978), 61, 111.

2. Augustine's famous treatise on the tension between the kingdom of God and earthly authorities is *City of God*.

3. See R. R. James, ed., *Winston S. Churchill: His Complete Speeches, 1897–1963* (New York: Chelsea House, 1974), 7:7566.

4. Solzhenitsyn, *World Split Apart*, 61.

5. Richard Rorty, "Religion as a Conversation-stopper," in *Philosophy and Social Hope* (New York: Penguin, 2000), 168–74. Christian philosopher Nicholas Wolterstorff responded to Rorty in "An Engagement with Rorty," *Journal of Religious Ethics* 31, no. 1 (Spring 2003): 129–39.

6. Václav Havel, *Disturbing the Peace: A Conversation with Karel Hvížďala*, trans. Paul Wilson (New York: Vintage, 1990), 11.

7. Dietrich Bonhoeffer, *Letters and Papers from Prison*, rev. ed., ed. Eberhard Bethge (New York: Macmillan, 1967), 17.

8. Cited in Rosetta E. Ross, *Witnessing and Testifying: Black Women, Religion, and Civil Rights* (Minneapolis: Fortress, 2003), v.

Chapter 2

1. See C. H. Lawrence, *Medieval Monasticism: Forms of Religious Life in Western Europe in the Middle Ages* (New York: Longman, 1984), 104.

2. Cicero discusses these three purposes in *De Optimo Genere Oratorum* (*On the Best Style of Orators*), I, 3; *Orator*, 69; and *De Oratore* (*On Oratory*), II, 28. Augustine affirms them in *De Doctrina Christiana* (*On Christian Doctrine*), 4.12.27.

3. A cautionary essay about Paul's use of rhetoric is Jeffrey A. D. Weima, "What Does Aristotle Have to Do with Paul? An Evaluation of Rhetorical Criticism," *Calvin Theological Journal* 32 (1997): 458–68.

4. Chrysostom's views on the importance of rhetorical education for Christians are addressed in Lauri Thurén, "John Chrysostom as a Rhetorical Critic: The Hermeneutics of an Early Father," *Biblical Interpretation* 9, no. 2 (2001): 183.

5. Augustine, *On Christian Doctrine*, 3.4.3.

6. The history of Christian rhetoricians' competition with other rhetoricians is discussed in David S. Cunningham, *Faithful Persuasion: In Aid of a Rhetoric of Christian Theology* (Notre Dame: University of Notre Dame Press, 1991), xiv. The critical importance of rhetoric for the early church is addressed in Averil Cameron, *Christianity and the Rhetoric of Empire: The Development of Christian Discourse* (Berkeley: University of California Press, 1991). For a short history of Christian rhetoric, see George A. Kennedy, *Classical Rhetoric and Its Christian and Secular Tradition from Ancient to Modern Times*, 2nd ed. (Chapel Hill: University of North Carolina Press, 1999).

7. For a contemporary discussion of the rhetoric of naming, see Thomas Conley, *Rhetoric in the European Tradition* (New York: Longman, 1990), 274.

8. Frank Spotnitz, "Sidney Poitier," *American Film* 16 (September/October 1991): 21.

9. The Hebrew word *dabar* is discussed in Walter J. Ong, *Orality and Literacy: The Technologizing of the Word* (London: Routledge, 1982), 75. The concept of speech as intentional action is developed in Nicholas Wolterstorff, *Divine Discourse: Philosophical Reflections on the Claim That God Speaks* (Cambridge: Cambridge University Press, 1995).

10. John L. Locke, *The De-Voicing of Society: Why We Don't Talk to Each Other Anymore* (New York: Simon & Schuster, 1998), 105.

Chapter 3

1. Mike Yaconelli, "Can We Talk?" *Wittenberg Door* 35, no. 197 (January/February 2005): 22.

2. Elie Wiesel, *And the Sea Is Never Full: Memoirs, 1969–*, trans. Marion Wiesel (New York: Knopf, 1999), 154.

3. Ibid.

4. Augustine, *On Christian Doctrine*, 3.19.29.

5. Augustine, *Confessions*, IV.i.1; III.iii.7.

6. Patrick Hart and Jonathan Montaldo, eds., *The Intimate Merton: His Life from His Journals* (San Francisco: HarperSanFrancisco, 1999), 106.

7. Pascal, *Pensées*, #44.

8. Dietrich Bonhoeffer, *Life Together*, trans. John W. Doberstein (New York: Harper & Row, 1954), 56.

9. Clifford Stoll, *High-Tech Heretic: Reflections of a Computer Contrarian* (New York: Anchor, 1999), 179.

10. See Ian Parker, "Absolute PowerPoint," *New Yorker*, May 28, 2001, 76–87.

11. Charles J. Chaput, "Fools with Tools Are Still Fools," *Nuntium* (June 1998), http://www.archden.org/archbishop/docs/foolswithtools.htm (accessed October 26, 2001).

Chapter 4

1. Knowing God's Word "by heart" originally meant learning it "by mouth" as well, since God's Word was read aloud rather than silently. See Jean Leclercq,

The Love of Learning and the Desire for God: A Study of Monastic Culture (New York: Fordham University Press, 1961), 3.

2. Augustine's *First Meanings in Genesis* describes some of the "first meanings" he believed were central to the Christian faith.

3. Nicholas Wolterstorff, *Reason within the Bounds of Religion*, 2nd ed. (Grand Rapids: Eerdmans, 1984), 76.

4. See George Herbert Wikramanayake, "A Note on the Meaning of *Pisteis* in Aristotle's Rhetoric," *American Journal of Philology* 82 (1961): 193–96; and Edward P. J. Corbett and Robert J. Connors, *Classical Rhetoric for the Modern Student* (New York: Oxford University Press, 1999), 493.

5. Walker Percy, *Signposts in a Strange Land*, ed. Patrick Samway (New York: Picador, 1991), 306.

6. Cited in Paul Strathern, *Kierkegaard in 90 Minutes* (Chicago: Ivan R. Dee, 1997), 80.

7. Augustine, *Confessions*, VII.vii.18.

8. Ibid., IX.iii.7.

9. Augustine, *On Christian Doctrine*, 4.27.60.

Chapter 5

1. Kenneth Burke, *The Rhetoric of Religion: Studies in Logology* (Berkeley: University of California Press, 1970), 288.

2. Augustine, *Expositions on the Book of Psalms*, ed. and trans. Philip Schaff (Grand Rapids: Eerdmans, 1956), 673.

3. Cited in Duc De Broglie, *Saint Ambrose*, trans. Margaret Maitland (London: Duckworth, 1899), 45.

4. Cicero, *De Oratore*, III.C.LIX.

5. Cited in Garry Wills, *Saint Augustine* (New York: Viking, 1999), 71.

6. Pascal, *Pensées*, #16.

Chapter 6

1. Tara May, "Unplugged: School Quiets Grad's Speech," *Grand Rapids Press*, May 20, 2004, A21, A31.

2. Augustine's strict prohibition against lying is discussed in Roger D. Ray, "Christian Conscience and Pagan Rhetoric: Augustine's Treatises on Lying," in *Studia Patristica*, vol. 22, ed. Elizabeth A. Livingstone (Leuven: Peeters Press, 1989), 321–25; and Paul J. Griffiths, *Lying: An Augustinian Theology of Duplicity* (Grand Rapids: Brazos, 2004).

3. Pascal, *Pensées*, #15.

4. Charles E. Moore, ed., *Provocations: Spiritual Writings of Kierkegaard* (Farmington, PA: Plough, 1999), 402.

5. For background on the development of early rhetoric in the courts, the forum, and the academy, see Edward P. J. Corbett and Robert J. Connors, *Classical Rhetoric for the Modern Student* (New York: Oxford University Press, 1999), 16, 490–91.

6. The negative connotation of the word *rhetoric* is discussed in David S. Cunningham, *Faithful Persuasion: In Aid of a Rhetoric of Christian Theology* (Notre Dame: University of Notre Dame Press, 1991), 9.

7. Augustine, *Confessions*, III.iii.6; IX.i.2. Augustine's disdain for "word vendors" is examined in Garry Wills, *Saint Augustine* (New York: Viking, 1999), 45.

Chapter 7

1. For background on the biblical concept of shalom, see Nicholas Wolterstorff, *Until Justice and Peace Embrace* (Grand Rapids: Eerdmans, 1983), 69–72.

2. Cicero, *De Oratore*, II.C.XXIX.

3. Aleksandr Solzhenitsyn, *A World Split Apart* (New York: Harper & Row, 1978), 27.

4. Cited in Charles E. Moore, ed., *Provocations: Spiritual Writings of Kierkegaard* (Farmington, PA: Plough, 1999), 19, 350.

5. Augustine, *On Christian Doctrine*, 3.2.1.

6. Eugene H. Peterson, *Christ Plays in Ten Thousand Places* (Winnipeg, Manitoba: CMBC Publications, 1999), 59.

7. Rabbi Joseph Telushkin, *Words That Hurt; Words That Heal: How to Use Words Wisely and Well* (New York: Perennial Current, 1998), xx.

A book-related website includes audio, video, and text examples of the principles of servant speaking (see www.quentinschultze .com). This website is updated regularly with the latest national and international speeches that students are likely to recognize. Send me an email (schu@calvin.edu) if you are interested in course syllabi, exams, quizzes, and classroom activities based on the material in this book. A network of colleagues using the book either as the sole or a supplemental text in college courses gladly shares these materials.